"Throughout my twenty-six years of flying airplanes chair flying or visualization as an aid for preparatio that details these techniques or procedures in the co

"In *Performance Pilot*, Phil and Ross have written that provides excellent information on how to prepa of these techniques to an expert level.

"This book is relevant to any recreational, professio own performance and skills. As a current instructor book I will recommend to all my students."

— Squadron Leader, Marq Saunders,
RAAF Fighter Combat Instructor

"As a 20-year US Air Force pilot, I have had the opportunity to fly large four-engine transport aircraft on all seven continents, from combat in Afghanistan to remote ice runways in Antarctica. Every flight demands the highest level of performance from the crew to ensure safe operations. As a military flight instructor, I have flown with pilots of all experience levels, from those with just 300 hours to others with over 10,000 hours. It is amazing to see the difference between pilots who prepare and those who don't. This book has techniques for all experience levels designed to help any pilot develop their skills and performance. For those just starting out, the techniques in this book can help create a foundation they can build upon and use throughout their flying career. In short, the strategies in this book can help build better pilots."

— Lieutenant Colonel, Brent Keenan,
USAF, C-17A Instructor Pilot and Squadron Commander

"There are plenty of books that describe the technical aspects of flying airplanes, but the human performance psychology has largely been ignored. Airlines are now investigating how human factors contribute to accidents and are spending huge amounts of time and money attempting to eliminate human-centered accidents, but there is very little information for pilots on how to improve on high performance skills needed for high-stress and high-workload types of piloting.

"This book addresses that gap and gives pilots an understanding of the best and most efficient techniques on improving their aircraft handling in a way that will garner real results without needing to turn a propeller.

"I only wish I had this book years ago."

— Anthony Crichton-Browne,
Airbus A320 Captain,
competition aerobatic pilot and aviation podcaster

"Using hindsight, I see that during my training as a military pilot, I actually utilized some of the strategies described in this book. However, my personal implementation was haphazard and lacked the methodical and deliberate implementation required to apply them in an effective manner. This book describes the structure needed to effectively apply these learning techniques as well as introducing many new and complementary ones I had not considered. I am sure that my aviation training and subsequent career would have benefited greatly had this text been available at the time."

— Jaimie Tilbrook,
Former RAAF C130 Hercules Captain

"As a Grade 1 Flight Instructor and glider pilot, there is something I take very seriously which is absolutely vital to all pilots: airmanship! Airmanship is the very first thing I talk about with students during flying lesson number one. One aspect of airmanship is the ongoing optimization of our safe practices by enhancing our existing knowledge. Reading and practicing the advice in *Performance Pilot* will help you to enhance your airmanship. I know that after any of my flying students or colleagues have read *Performance Pilot*, I will sleep better in knowing that their flying careers will take them much more safely throughout their local skies and beyond."

— Andrew Musca-Unger,
Grade 1 Flight Instructor and glider pilot

ROSS BENTLEY • PHIL WILKES

PERFORMANCE PILOT

SKILLS, TECHNIQUES, AND STRATEGIES TO MAXIMIZE YOUR FLYING PERFORMANCE

Copyright © 2017 by Ross Bentley and Phil Wilkes

All rights reserved.
ISBN-13: 978-1507861585
ISBN-10: 1507861583
Library of Congress Control Number: 2015900566
CreateSpace Independent Publishing Platform, North Charleston, SC

Permission requests, trade and bulk order queries can be forwarded to:
info@performancepilot.net

"Aviation in itself is not inherently dangerous. But to an even greater degree than the sea, it is terribly unforgiving of any carelessness, incapacity or neglect."   - Captain A. G. Lamplugh

The information in this book is true and complete to the best of our knowledge. The advice contained within this book is made without any guarantee on the part of the authors, who disclaim any responsibility for your actions or results while applying any of the ideas, procedures or advice contained within.

Model names and designations mentioned herein are the property of the trademark holder and are used for identification purposes only. This is not an official publication.

Airbus A380 photograph courtesy Qantas Airways Limited
Cirrus SR22 photograph courtesy Cirrus Aircraft
F-35 Lightning II photograph courtesy Lockheed Martin Aeronautics
Kirby Chambliss & Jason Resop photograph courtesy Team Chambliss
Airbus A330 touch panel posters courtesy www.flightvectors.com
Procedural trainer photograph courtesy of Aerosim Technologies

Artwork by MazArt Design (mazartdesigns@netspace.net.au)
Editing by Red Herring Ink (robin@redherringink.com)

CONTENTS

Introduction	7
How The Pilot's Mind Works	12
Brain Integration	18
Sensory Input	26
Mental Programming	47
Mental Imagery	53
Learning	71
Self-Coaching	92
Preparation And Practice	97
Performance State Of Mind	101
Belief System	119
The Inner Game Of Flying	127
Pilot As Athlete	137
Cockpit Comfort	146
The Peak Performance Pilot	150
Appendix A: Performance Tips	154
Appendix B: Self-Coaching	155
Appendix C: Resources	159
Acknowledgements	159
Summary	160
About The Authors	162
Index	164

Introduction

Flying an aircraft is something learned mostly through hands-on experience; it's putting hours in your log book. You may have heard pilots say, or may have even said yourself, "All I need are more hours in my log book - more hours to develop the feel and skills to fly consistently at my peak." Sure, there is some truth in this statement, but to simply "sit around" in the pilot's seat and wait for the logged hours to give you the feel and the skills is time wasted.

You don't need to be sitting in an aircraft to take steps to improve your skills. You can make great leaps in developing and improving your skill level by utilizing the strategies presented in this book in preparation for your next venture into the wild-blue yonder. Effective preparation strategies away from the cockpit allow you to learn more quickly once you're behind the controls. If you understand the theory, if you can picture it clearly in your head before you start to fly, you will be more sensitive and able to relate to the experience and will learn to fly with proficiency much sooner. You may save years of trial and error learning (and dollars on flying lessons) by simply reading and understanding this book.

Any respectable flying instructor can teach you an attitude for straight and level, advise you where to aim during final approach to land, how much anticipation is required to level off from a climb or descent, or even how to fly accurately on a limited panel in instrument conditions. This book aims to add the mental game of flying and, most important, practice strategies that will get you to proficiency more quickly.

Once they've learned the basics, many pilots believe that all that separates them being the next World Aerobatics Champion, the next Red Bull ace, the next Chuck Yeager, or the next Chesley "Sully" Sullenberger is more flying hours - more practice. However, the message you'll hear from us a lot throughout this book is that practicing the same thing over and over doesn't guarantee success. Most of us know the adage, "A sure sign of insanity is doing the same thing over and over again and expecting something to change," but that's what pilots do all the time! They fly around and around, logging flying hours, expecting to improve. The fact that they sometimes do improve is more luck than anything else. It's also why many pilots do not improve as much as they could and, in some cases, actually get worse. In fact, practicing the wrong thing will only make you better at doing the wrong thing.

If football and basketball teams practiced like some pilots, they would show up and play a game each time, but they don't do they? Instead, their coaches break the game down into deliberate practice exercises, called drills, and only now and then do they play a full game. This book is meant to help you do that same thing with your flying. It's meant to break the act of flying down into deliberate practice strategies. When you put these drills together in your next flight, lesson, aerobatics sequence or simulator session, you'll perform better.

Have you ever wondered how much of flying is mental and how much is physical? If you are like most pilots, there are days when everything goes just right, when you are "in the groove" or "God's gift to aviation." Then there are other times when nothing seems to go right; you are so far behind the aircraft there are fingernail marks on the horizontal stabilizer. What makes the difference? Is it something you ate? Are you coming down with something? Are you distracted by noise from your life outside of flying? Is it physical? Is it the weather? Is it air traffic control's fault? Many things can play a role in how well you fly, but the prime determinant of your performance level in the cockpit is "mental." What does this mean? More importantly, what can you do about it? How can you increase the frequency of your peak performances and minimize the less-than-special days?

While flying obviously involves physical skill, at the same time, your body doesn't do anything without being told to by your brain. There is, therefore, a mental aspect to everything you do when flying an aircraft. This book seeks to address these mental aspects.

Our main goal is to help you learn more in a shorter period. Left on your own, you will gain experience and improve your abilities. Our hope is that this book will speed up that process so that you can learn in one session what may have taken multiple sessions if relying solely on getting more hours in your log book.

Hopefully, we are preaching to the converted since you probably wouldn't be reading this book if you didn't think there was something more to be gained from using mental strategies to improve your flying. For that, we congratulate you and strongly encourage you never to lose that mindset; the mindset that there is always more to learn, always more to improve in your flying, and always more fun to be had.

Whether you are an amateur or a professional, a student pilot or experienced aviator, a general-aviation pilot, flying instructor, competition aerobatic pilot, air-race pilot, military pilot or airline pilot, this book is written for you. Our hope for this book is that it will give you the tools and background to analyze how to maximize your level of performance on a consistent basis and to have a successful and enjoyable career whatever level you choose to take your aviating to.

If you are a student pilot, this book will serve as reference material on your journey to becoming an experienced and proficient aviator. Reading and using the information in this book may help you develop your basic skills without acquiring bad habits. That will give you an edge as your career progresses, cutting down the time needed to reach proficiency as you can concentrate totally on improving rather than dealing with bad habits. Some of the information may not make sense until you've gone past the basics and begun working on fine-tuning your techniques, but hopefully it will help you start on the right foot and then you can refer to it later.

For the experienced pilot, there may be a lot of information you already know, some of which you may be using without even understanding why. We suggest you read it again and thoroughly think it through. It's surprising how a fresh approach can sometimes make it all click for you, resulting in a dramatic increase in performance.

The strategies we will present are easy to implement, but it's up to you to do it. After all, you can have all the information in the world, but if you don't do anything with it, your performance will never improve. You may feel a bit awkward or uncomfortable at first using some of the strategies we suggest here. Don't worry; you're not the only one. If this is you, there are always ways and places to do them where you won't feel that way. Once you start performing at your very best on a consistent basis, we're sure everyone around you will want to know what your secret is.

Some of the strategies we suggest may not seem or feel "right" to you, while others will. Use the ones that feel right immediately and try the others now and then making a note of the changes in your performance over time. Just because a strategy doesn't feel right or seem to be making a difference immediately, it doesn't mean you should dismiss it completely. The more strategies you use on a regular basis, the better a pilot you will be.

Using the strategies presented in this book requires a commitment. Motivation and commitment can be developed more easily when you believe that what you are doing will be effective. This belief, however, is subject to your understanding of the process. Without that understanding, few people will accept the strategies. That is why we will explain the whys and hows in this book. The better you understand the concepts, the stronger your belief in their effectiveness will be, and the stronger your motivation will be to use them.

Evidence of some success is also necessary to provide continued motivation, but without implementing these strategies, there can be no evidence. We have all heard people say, "I tried that once, and it didn't work" or "I knew it wouldn't work!" If you'd witnessed the success we've achieved with pilots and athletes utilizing the strategies presented, you would have all the evidence and motivation you need. You may be able to argue about the theory of something, but when you see and experience the results, there is no argument. Once you begin to use these strategies, you will experience firsthand the results and gain all the motivation you need to continue.

Throughout the book, you will find Performance Tips that serve as memory jogs for the most important concepts covered. You can flip open to most pages and pick up something that's meaningful and helpful to you.

Implement Strategies

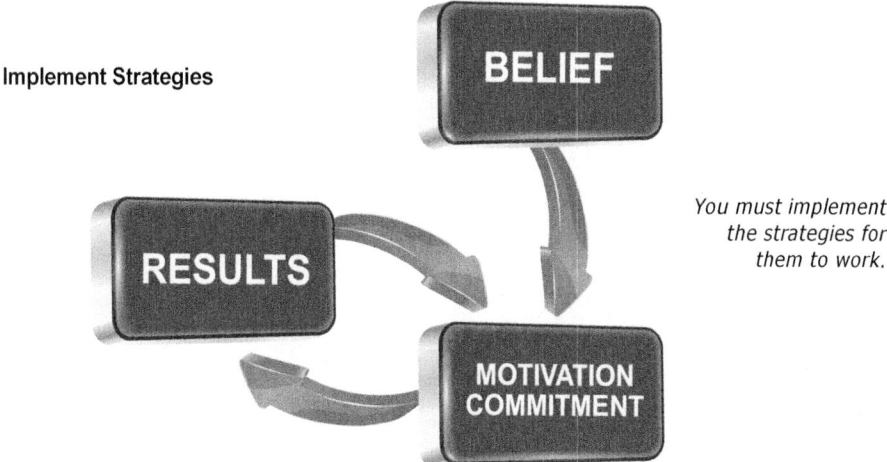

You must implement the strategies for them to work.

This book means to act as a tool for pilots who want to operate at a peak level of performance. The one thing we know for sure is that if you don't use what we write about in this book, it won't help you at all. It's as simple as that.

It's one thing to read a book, but an entirely other matter to put to use what you've read. This book is not one to read once and place on a shelf. Our hope is that you'll refer to it on a regular basis throughout your career, keeping it nearby, either at home or in your nav bag.

To assist your ongoing use of our book, we have included a summary at the end. A larger scale version of the summary can also be downloaded from our website (www.performancepilot.net/summary) and laminated so you can use it as a guide to all of the important strategies within the book.

How The Pilot's Mind Works

Yogi Berra, the famous US baseball player, coach and manager, said, "Baseball is 90% mental; the other half is physical." If you ignore the math, you could have equally made this comment about flying. The physical act of flying an aircraft is relatively simple in comparison with the mental aspects. In other words, your results are largely dependent upon your mental performance.

If you want to perform at your peak while flying, having an understanding of how your mind works is not only beneficial, it is critical. The goal of this chapter is to give you enough information so that you will buy into the concepts and tools we want you to use. Without this basic understanding, it is doubtful you will believe in the concepts and, therefore, will not use them. With this as a framework, let's dive into the pilot's mind.

The Performance Model

Ronn Langford, Ross's friend, developed The Performance Model. It's used to explain and understand how humans perform practically any activity. The model works like this: information, primarily from our senses, is input into our brains, which we can look at as operating like a computer. In this "bio-computer," the information is processed based on our software or programming, resulting in output. When it comes to flying an aircraft, this output is some form of action or reaction: using the control column or rudder pedals, looking at something, making a decision, behaving a certain way, having self-confidence or millions of other actions.

Within your software, or mental programming, are your psychomotor skills (physical actions and movements that you can do without having conscious thought), your state of mind, decisions, behavioral traits and your belief system.

You could have the latest and greatest supercomputer, with the very best software or programming available, but if the input you give it is of poor quality or very little quantity, you will not get the output you were seeking. Conversely, if you give an old computer, with a slow processor, lots of great quality input, you still will not get the output you were looking for (at least not as quickly as is needed when flying). In other words, the combination of your brain's processing speed and your software (programming) determine the output which, in this case, is your flying performance.

The Performance Model.

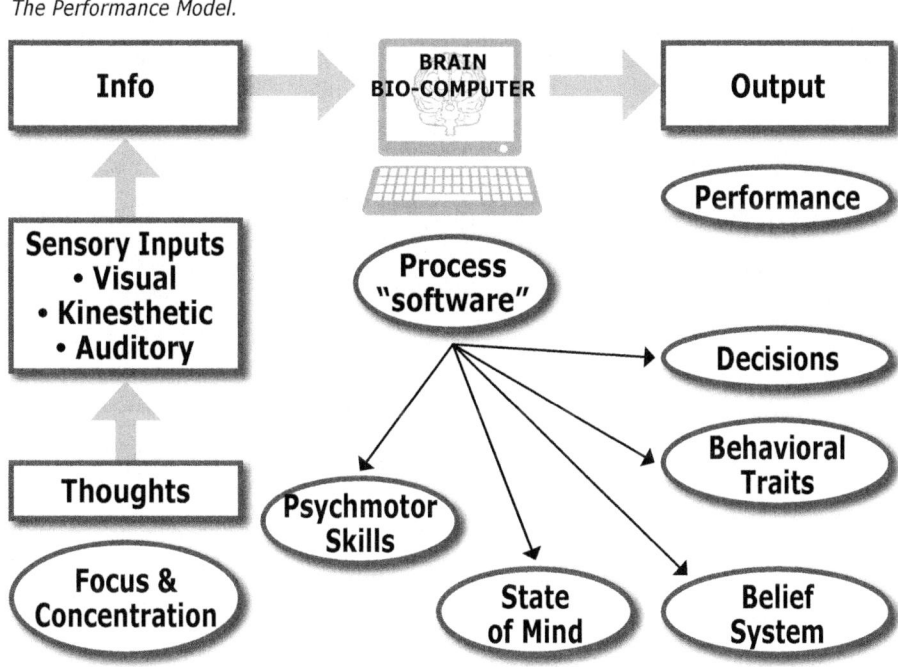

Using Your Whole Brain

Have you ever had days or times when you feel completely switched on and performing at a high level and other days when it seems you can't get out of your own way? Part of the reason for this is how well you're using your whole brain. When you switch on and are performing at your best, you're using your whole brain and processing information quickly and efficiently. When you're not performing well, it's as if you're only using half a brain; you're not processing information very fast.

It's surprising to many pilots that they can use some exercises to speed up their brain's ability to process information and therefore fly more proficiently and smarter. We'll look into brain integration and how you can improve your brain's functioning in the next chapter.

Sensory Information

Anyone familiar with computers will have heard the saying "garbage in, garbage out" or "GIGO" for short. The same thing applies to our minds; if we input garbage, the output will be garbage. Of course, the opposite is also true: "quality in, quality out."

So where do you get the information that is input into your brain? From two main sources: sensory input and thoughts. Sensory inputs can be broken down further into visual, kinesthetic, and auditory. Since the only use of your sense of smell when flying is to deal with problems (e.g., smoke or fumes), and not to improve your performance, we'll not deal with it in this book. Of course, we don't use our sense of taste while flying (except eating crew meals!).

Most of the information you put into your brain when flying comes visually. What is not so obvious is exactly what visual means. To many people, having 20/20 vision means having good visual input. While central vision acuity, which is what the 20/20 measurement relates to, is important it is not the most important part of the visual input. For example, visual-spatial awareness, peripheral vision, depth perception, and the ability to change focal points rapidly are much more critical to flying. That is why some pilots with 20/20 vision do not "see" as much as others who have lesser vision.

The kinesthetic sense involves much more than just the sense of touch. It also includes your proprioceptive system (the ability to sense forces acting against your body) and your vestibular system (sense of balance).

Is your sense of balance important to flying an aircraft? Is your ability to sense the g-forces against your body important? Is your ability to feel the control forces being fed back through the yoke, stick, pedals and seat important? Yes, yes, and yes!

> **PERFORMANCE TIP**
> *The better the quality and the more quantity of input from your senses that you can process, the better the output and the better your performance will be.*

Some people seem to think that auditory input is not that important when it comes to flying aircraft. It is true that our auditory sense is the first to suffer when we are mentally overloaded. If you don't believe us, consider how many radio calls you have missed while concentrating intently on just flying or how many times your spouse has accused you of selective hearing! Having said that, a great pilot still receives a lot of input from their hearing. At your most aware, you just know when you are getting a little slow turning final or are approaching the stall as your auditory senses pick up the decreasing sound of the air rushing past the cockpit. The sound of the engine tells you a lot about whether your throttle adjustment was in the ballpark. Sounds out of the ordinary pinpoint our errors for us; we haven't moved the propeller control to fine pitch on final, we left the gear down after take-off or forgot to select it down on final!

A pilot's primary sensory inputs come from their eyes, ears and touch.

The overall message you should be getting from this is that anything you can do to improve the quantity and quality of sensory information going into your brain the better your performance will be. We'll get into the details of how exactly to do this in the chapter on Sensory Input.

Your Software

Everything you do behind the controls of the aircraft (and in life for that matter) is a result of the programming in your brain. What do we mean by programming? Each and every time you do something, anything, the synapses in your brain that relate to that activity fire off bio-electrical current from one to another. This pathway now becomes the program for doing this act. The more often the act is completed, the deeper the programming becomes.

Let us make one thing very clear; you must fly an aircraft at the subconscious level and not the conscious level. Why? The aviation environment is far too dynamic for an aircraft to be flown effectively at the conscious level. A pilot cannot think through each skill and technique as they fly the aircraft. Let's consider the captain of a jet airliner conducting a take-off at the distance-limited performance weight limit from a contaminated runway. Imagine now that the captain is rejecting the take-off close to V1. Imagine them thinking themselves through the entire process. "Ok! Start braking now by moving my feet up onto the brakes and squeezing them down together while keeping the aircraft straight with rudder, simultaneously moving my right hand to the reverse thrust levers and applying maximum reverse thrust suitable for the conditions while being prepared to use asymmetric thrust on the applicable side if we start to aquaplane on this contaminated runway...." Where do you think they would end up? Quite possibly in a post-crash investigation into why they took so long to complete the reject actions as they were sliding off the end of the runway!

To emphasize the importance of flying at the subconscious level, consider this fact: your conscious mind processes information at a rate of 2,000 bits of data per second while your subconscious mind processes at a rate of four billion bits of data per second! Is there any wonder why the subconscious is better at operating in such a dynamic environment?

You must rely on, and trust, your subconscious programming to fly the aircraft. From where does that programming originate? Mostly from experience and physical programming, but it can also come from mental programming. We most often hear this mental programming referred to as visualization or mental imagery.

Virtually every pilot will have been told, at some stage of their training, of the virtues of practicing sequences to be flown using bedroom or armchair flying, i.e., using some form of visualization technique to rehearse. Most pilots will even tell you that they use visualization when a majority of them just close their eyes and think about what they want to achieve. Effective mental programming is more than just that. Mental imagery is in reality "actualization" where a person uses all their senses and not only their visual sense. They not only imagine what a scenario looks like but also how it feels and sounds. The more senses they use in their mental imagery, and the more real they can make it, the more effective a tool it will be.

The Three Keys to Improving Flying Performance

Based on The Performance Model, you can see there are three keys to improving your flying performance:

- Faster Processing – The faster and more efficiently you process the information in your brain, the better your performance will be.

- Quality Input – The better the quality and the more quantity of input from your senses that you can process, the better the output and the better your performance will be.

- Quality Programming – The better your mental programming (your software) is, the better your performance will be.

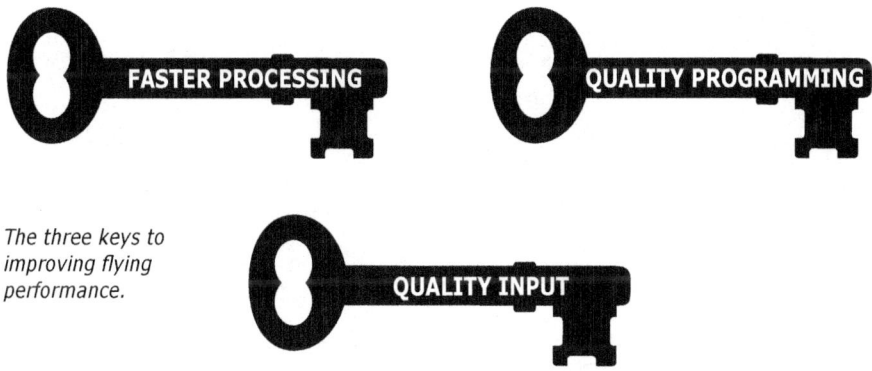

The three keys to improving flying performance.

Because these are so critical to your performance, we're devoting the next four chapters to discussing methods you can use to improve in these three areas.

Brain Integration

You are most likely aware of the fact that your brain is made up of two halves or hemispheres. Each hemisphere has certain primary responsibilities: the left hemisphere for logic, math, language, and details; the right for creativity, intuition, art and the big picture.

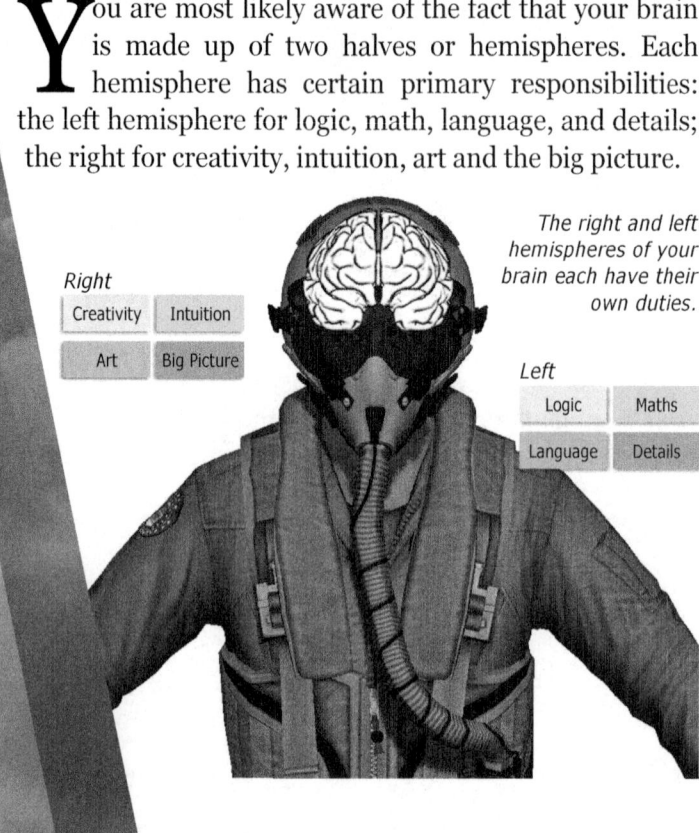

The right and left hemispheres of your brain each have their own duties.

Right
- Creativity
- Intuition
- Art
- Big Picture

Left
- Logic
- Maths
- Language
- Details

How would you describe yourself? Are you a left-brain dominant person; logical, factual, and detail-oriented? Or are you more right-brain dominant; creative, intuitive, and able to see the big picture?

Which do you suppose is the ideal for a pilot? If you answered "both" you are correct. You must be able to see the details and the big picture, be logical and creative, factual, and intuitive. You must be what is called "integrated;" both hemispheres of your brain working at their peak and together. In fact, sports researchers have shown that one of the most important factors leading to an athlete performing "in the zone" or "in the flow" is having a fully-integrated mind.

Between the two hemispheres of your brain is a bundle of nerve fibers called the corpus callosum. The corpus callosum acts as a communications link transferring bio-electrical current between the hemispheres, much like the function of a network cable between two computers.

It is as if there is a dimmer switch in this communications link - one that can dial up or down the amount of bio-electrical communication between the hemispheres. When the communication is restricted, you act either more left-brained or more right-brained. When the communication is turned up, you are integrated. That is what leads to great performances; that's when you fly at your best.

The left hemisphere controls the right side of the body, and the right hemisphere controls the left side of the body. At least that is the way it should be. Some people, and thus some pilots, do not operate completely in this manner. Instead - at least partially - their right hemisphere controls the right side of their body and vice versa. Dis-integration can lead to a lack of coordination as the brain and body are not operating together at their peak.

You will think more "whole-brained" and perform in a more coordinated fashion when you are fully integrated. Fortunately, we can improve our level of integration training by using the following exercises.

Cross-Crawl

As we mentioned, the right hemisphere of your brain controls the left side of your body and vice versa. There is, or at least should be, cross lateral communication from one side of the body to the opposite side of the brain. This communication occurs at a high level when you are integrated and not so much when you are less integrated (i.e., dis-integrated).

Almost any physical movement that connects one side of the body with the other will help your level of brain integration. However, the simple cross-crawl exercise may be the most effective. Here's how it works:

While standing, raise your right leg, bending it at the knee, and bring your left arm over and touch the right knee. Return to standing. Then raise your left leg and touch the knee with your right hand. Return to standing, and then continue, alternating sides. Keep your head facing forward, but let your eyes follow the path of your hands as they touch each knee. You will find yourself marching in one place while alternately touching your knees with your opposite hands. Cross-crawls are a lot like marching on the spot, so all you military pilots should be good at this one!

The cross-crawl exercise.

At first, do this at what is a comfortable rate for you and then slow it down to the slowest pace you can. Doing it at a slow pace puts more stress on your sense of balance, improving it over time. Then speed it up until you are almost running on the spot while touching the opposite knee with your hands. At speed, this is a great exercise to get your body warmed up before getting into the aircraft.

There is a reason this exercise is called a cross-crawl. When babies first begin to crawl they most often do it in a unilateral motion; they move their right hand and leg forward, then their left hand and leg and so on; one side moves and then the other. After a week (or more for most babies) they change to a cross-lateral crawling movement where they move the right hand with the left leg, then the left hand with the right leg and so on. This cross-crawling movement is the first step in the integration process of brain development.

Children who don't do enough cross-crawling (often because they go almost directly from unilateral crawling to walking) may miss out on becoming fully integrated at an early age. In many cases, this leads to the child being slightly uncoordinated or even having what some people call learning disabilities. By simply using the cross-crawl exercise many children have been able to "recover" from learning difficulties and have become far more physically coordinated. This exercise is extremely powerful.

Do cross-crawls for about 30 seconds each morning, in the evening, and especially just before getting into the aircraft. After doing this for a few weeks, you will begin to be aware of when you need to become more integrated by doing more cross-crawls. You will just feel better - more in the zone - when you're integrated. For the self-conscious, there are many "more private" places you can perform cross-crawls before flying: in a quiet corner of the airline or flying school car-park, an empty briefing room, or behind a hangar door. We would urge you to trust and persist with all of the techniques presented in this book, but if you are looking for something a little less obvious, or even something to do in addition to cross-crawls, then the next exercise is a good one.

Head and Eye Motion Integration

As you sit in the cockpit or flight deck, do a combination of the following actions:

- With your eyes, look to the left while at the same time moving your head to the right,

- With your eyes, look to the right while at the same time moving your head to the left,

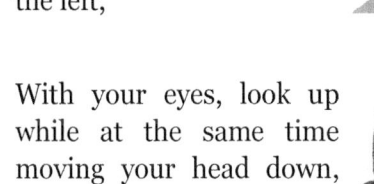

- With your eyes, look up while at the same time moving your head down, and

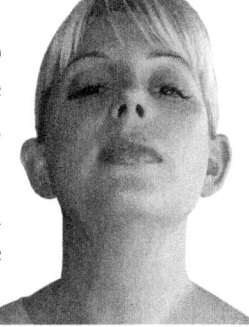

- With your eyes, look down while at the same time moving your head up.

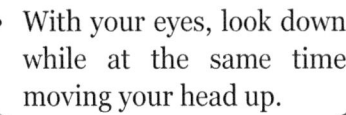

Randomize the order you do these actions and vary the speed at which you do them. This exercise is a lot harder than it sounds, but once you have been doing it for a couple of minutes (and your brain starts to be integrated), you will notice that it becomes easier. Continue the exercise until you can consistently do it without error and your brain has become integrated. You have now set yourself up for a great performance.

Lazy-8s

The following integration exercise is especially effective in helping integrate your vision. Just as there is a cross lateral connection between your brain and body, there is a similar connection between your brain and eyes. In this case, the information coming into your right eye is sent primarily to the left hemisphere of your brain and the information from your left eye is sent primarily to your right hemisphere. Once it is in your brain, the information is processed and constructed into what you "see."

If communication between your eyes and brain and from hemisphere to hemisphere is in any way restricted, you may miss a piece of the picture. At the speed you're traveling in the aircraft, missing just the tiniest piece of information could be catastrophic. Believe us when we say that a large percentage of the population, even professional pilots, have visual processing problems resulting in incomplete visual pictures. You see it on your drive to the airport with drivers making the wrong decisions when trying to cut between two cars while overtaking. As for a pilot-specific example, it is those small errors of turning final too late and overshooting the runway centerline or misjudging your flare height and thumping on the landing. These may be the ultimate result of a visual processing problem that the lazy-8s exercise can help correct.

Here's how it works. Stand with one arm stretched directly out in front of you with a slight bend in your elbow and your hand in the thumbs-up position. Trace an imaginary figure eight lying on its side (that's where the "lazy-8s" name comes from) with your thumb while you keep your head steady; follow your thumb with your eyes. Your eyes will track this lazy-8 (or infinity) figure.

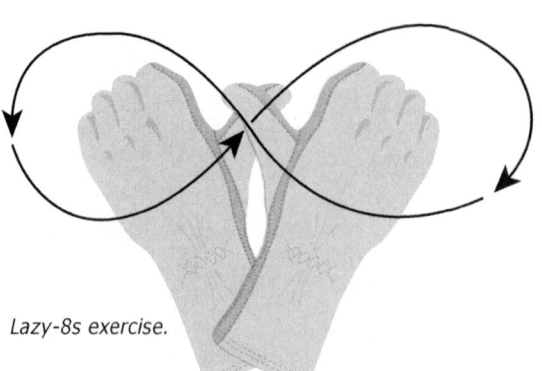

Lazy-8s exercise.

Do this exercise for about 20 to 30 seconds with each hand and then with both hands. When doing it with both hands, make two fists, place the knuckles from each hand together, and make a cross with your two thumbs. While flexing your arms and shoulders, trace the lazy-8s while focusing on the cross of your two thumbs. Again, make sure your head stays steady.

At first, have someone watch your eyes closely while you do this. Do they move smoothly and congruently (together)? Or are they "notchy;" jumping ahead in certain areas and skipping parts of the figure eight? If so, they may be missing information in that area of your visual field.

If your eyes do have some "notchiness," jumping or incongruence in tracking doing some lazy-8s for even 30 seconds to a minute will probably begin to make some improvement. Even if you didn't notice any problems with the way your eyes track, this exercise would benefit you. Again, it helps with brain integration and, specifically, visual integration.

Most people seem to think that good vision is something you are either born with or not and that it's something that just goes away with age. Yet they will agree that if a person does some form of physical exercise, their body will stay healthy for a longer period. The same thing applies to a person's vision; if you exercise your vision, it will improve and maintain its health and performance level longer.

You should do this exercise at least twice a day and especially just before getting into the aircraft. Ross has used these exercises while coaching race car drivers and many report an immediate effect. They say it helps them become more aware of what is going on around them and be much more perceptive. The resulting awareness and perception obviously help improve the quality of visual information being input into their brains.

Centering

How important is it to the overall performance of the aircraft that rudder input is used to balance adverse aileron yaw in turns? It's very important, right? Even if the aircraft is perfectly balanced, if your personal sense of balance is not near-perfect, are you going to be able to fly the aircraft to its optimal performance? Or, if the aircraft is not perfectly balanced, and neither are you, how effective are you going to be at exactly interpreting what the aircraft needs to restore balance?

Any instrument-rated pilot who has experienced "the leans" will know that your sense of balance is as critical as the aircraft's and if your sense of balance is disturbed, you need to take action to restore it. In a case of "the leans," we accomplish this by trusting our instruments until our brain has a chance to make sense of everything and restores our sense of balance. So, if we can agree that our sense of balance is vital to operating at peak performance, can we improve our sense of balance? Yes. How? One way is by "centering."

Centering is a technique that has been used by Tibetan monks for over 2,000 years, in the martial arts, and more recently by sports psychologists. One centering technique involves pressing a couple of fingers from one hand upon your navel and focusing all your attention on this center point of the body.

Another centering technique is to lightly press the tip of your tongue to the roof of your mouth towards the front behind your upper teeth (where peanut butter sticks!). This area in a person's mouth is a strong acupressure point which triggers brain integration and an improved sense of balance. You could even try centering while doing cross-crawls!

Obviously, you cannot fly the aircraft while pressing your navel, but you can place the tip of your tongue on the roof of your mouth, particularly at times of high workload or stress. When approaching decision altitude on an ILS approach, trying to make very small changes to the flight path to remain on the localizer and glideslope while at the same time avoiding pilot-induced oscillations, center (placing your tongue on the roof of your mouth) and breathe. Just before you taxi out onto the runway for take-off, center. Before you disconnect the autopilot for a hand-flown approach, center. Before your first solo or on your flight test, center. By centering when you most need to be integrated, sensitive to what the aircraft is telling you, and balanced, you will be.

This centering technique also has a stress-relieving or relaxing effect. An uptight, stressed-out pilot will rarely perform at their peak. By centering you will be more relaxed, learn at a quicker rate, and perform at your best more consistently. By practicing centering regularly, you

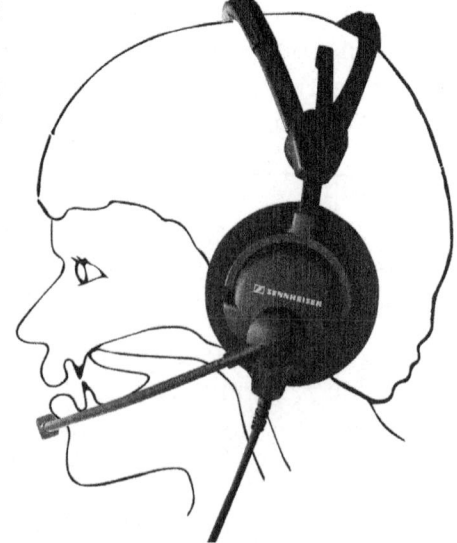

Center yourself by placing your tongue on the roof of your mouth.

will notice a difference in and out of the aircraft. Over a short period, this will trigger a calm, focused, integrated brain.

Ask yourself, when could centering help you?

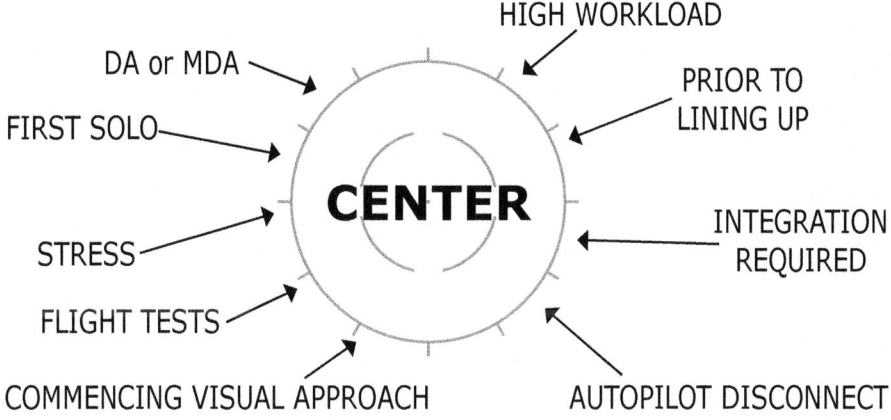

Sensory Input

Most people would agree that hand-eye coordination is a very important part of flying an aircraft, but few could give you a clue as to how to improve it. Here is what hand-eye coordination is: your brain processes information fed to it through your eyes and then your hand (or any other part of your body) is instructed to perform the appropriate action. From this simple explanation, it is easy to see why any improvement in the quality or quantity of the information going from your eyes to your brain should result in a more "coordinated" action.

On the other hand, imagine trying to fly an aircraft with restricted sensory input. Imagine trying to maintain the ideal approach path if you restricted your vision by 90%. Isn't this similar to what we do when we learn to fly on instruments while wearing the hood or "under the bag?" Restricting all peripheral vision deprives our brain of its major source of sensory input, and we are forced to be totally reliant on our instruments for information. We have to expend a great deal of concentration to generate the same level of situational awareness that we have with unobstructed vision in clear skies. As the old saying implies, "a peek is worth a thousand scans!"

What if your body was completely isolated from the aircraft so that you could not feel any of the vibrations, g-forces, roll, or pitch? What if you were deaf and couldn't hear any sound whatsoever from the aircraft? Would that affect your ability to fly the aircraft at your peak? Absolutely!

Every decision or physical movement you make is the result of the little pieces of information entering your brain from your senses (primarily vision, feel, and hearing when it comes to flying). As we established in our discussion of the pilot's mind, the better the quality and the more quantity of input from your senses that you can process, the better the output and the better your performance will be.

Visual Input

Have you ever wondered whether what you see is what other people see? Have you wondered whether what you see or perceive to be the color red is the same as what other people see or perceive as red? Have you ever wondered whether other pilots see as much or more than you do? Why is it that some pilots seem to be all seeing, all aware, all knowing of everything going on around them when other pilots seem to be wearing blinders?

Most people think it is your eyes that provide you with what you see, where, in reality, it is more your brain. What you see is primarily what your brain constructs. In other words, your brain is sent a small amount of data by your eyes and it turns it into a lot of useful information. Vision researchers have proved this point. That is why some people with 20/20 eyesight "see" more than others with 20/20 eyesight. Some older pilots, whose eyesight may not be as good as younger pilots', see and are aware of more.

Some pilots pick up traffic miles away without even being told about it; maybe from a tiny flash of something in their peripheral vision. For others that same amount of data from the eyes results in little to no visual construction in the brain; they don't assimilate the information. That, of course, is why some pilots seem to be able to see any traffic in their vicinity while others can't pick it up even after ATC has given notice of crossing flight paths. It's just that these pilots are not able to make any useful sense out of the minuscule amount of data sent to their brain by their eyes.

Think of a pilot who has a reputation for flying out of the slot on final approach and making a lot of bad landings as a result. To most observers, it is simply a matter of prioritization and not concentrating hard enough on slot retention. The cause of the problem may instead be due to a lack of quality sensory input, especially visual input. For instance, where most pilots on final approach may recognize that the aim point has started to move in the windshield instead of staying fixed, our "visually challenged" pilot doesn't pick this up. The reason is that, for a fraction of a second, they do not see the whole picture. Whatever the reason, there was a restriction with their visual input.

It would only take a very small piece of the puzzle to be missing for an error to occur at flying speeds. When you think about it with this in mind, you can see why some pilots fly less accurately or consistently than others and why they seem to make more than their fair share of bad decisions.

Fortunately, you can develop your visual processing. How? Firstly, you can do this by using the lazy-8s exercise recommended in the previous chapter. You will be amazed at the improvement in your visual sense if you use these exercises on a regular basis. Secondly, a short period of sensory deprivation can lead to an increase in sensitivity.

Consider for a moment a blind person. Are their other senses (feel, hearing, taste, smell) usually more or less sensitive than people with sight? Better, right? Why is that? Because they have been forced to develop the senses they have. Any time you focus on one specific sensory input, it will become more sensitive. If you could get airborne blindfolded, and survive, imagine how much you could improve your other senses (Note: in NO way do we advocate wearing a blindfold as a strategy to improve your flying!).

By restricting some of your senses for a short period you force your brain to assimilate greater input from your other senses, and they become much more sensitive. Of course, it is not something you consciously set about doing; it is something your mind automatically does on its own. We can use a strategy based on this premise to develop the visual construction process.

If you restrict the amount of information your eyes can send to your brain but ask your brain for just as much information output, it is up to your brain to make up the difference. In other words, send your brain a little bit of data and expect your brain to output a lot of information. Now we can probably all agree that going flying with your vision even slightly restricted is dangerous. But what if you practiced taking the same amount of data from your eyes as you usually do, while asking your brain to output more information using that little data? What you are doing, in fact, is practicing being more aware; practicing using your brain's vision construction abilities; and practicing being sensitive to visual data.

It is, in fact, something you can and should practice not only with your flying. It is something you can practice while driving on the street and also in all other activities in your life. For example, while driving down the highway on your way to the airport (in fact the more often, the better) and using your vision as you normally do, ask your brain for as much information as possible. Ask it to be aware of everything along the side of the roadway. Make a note of the ground, the grass, and the trees in great detail as you pass by, but don't just take notice of the amount of them. Note the color, type, and amount of leaves on the trees, the condition of the bark, whether the ground is made up of mostly dirt or rocks, etc., and the speed at which they pass.

When doing this, don't look directly at the ground, grass, and trees. Look down the road like you normally would, but allow your brain to take in more peripheral information (actually construct more information from the data your eyes are supplying to it). While driving in traffic on the street practice being aware of every car, truck, pedestrian, and anything else. Ask your brain to provide more information. There is a physical limit to how much your eyes can take in, but it is practically limitless what your brain can do with that information.

Practice taking in more visual information.

Think also of all the situations in your flying where you can complete a similar exercise: joining a busy traffic pattern (i.e., a circuit for those from the Commonwealth of Nations), turning onto the base leg of the pattern, coming in to land, pulling up from a loop. You are surely able to think up dozens of examples. Imagine yourself looking where you normally look, but noticing so much more around you. Noticing more is the goal of this exercise. The example of coming in to land is one Phil has used personally to try and improve the consistency of his flare height.

> **PERFORMANCE TIP**
> *Every day, practice being aware.*

What you are doing here is practicing becoming more aware of everything around you while using the same amount of visual data supplied by your eyes. Practicing this in your everyday world will greatly enhance your performance in the air. The more you practice this, the more aware you will be of everything happening around you in the cockpit or on the flight deck and in the air without having to put much, if any, concentration on it.

One of the more difficult visual challenges you may face is seeing a long way ahead of the aircraft. Often your view is restricted by atmospheric conditions: cloud, haze, fog. If you consciously try to stretch your vision, trying to look as far ahead as possible (even if it means using your imagination), over and over again when practicing, eventually it will become a habit or a mental program. Then, it will be something that you do without any conscious thought. It's as if you are building a mental picture to fill in the holes in the visual picture.

A great example of this is when you pre-brief what lights you are expecting to see when you break visual from an instrument approach and where the runway will be in the windscreen.

Another example is taking off in low visibility conditions and consciously building a mental picture of how the runway ahead of you would look if you were actually in CAVOK (Ceiling and Visibility OK) conditions. The A330 captain who gave Phil this example swears that this mental picture helps him with runway centerline retention in reduced visibility.

At all times, you are receiving information from the aircraft. The more sensitive you are to receiving that feedback, the more able you will be to fly

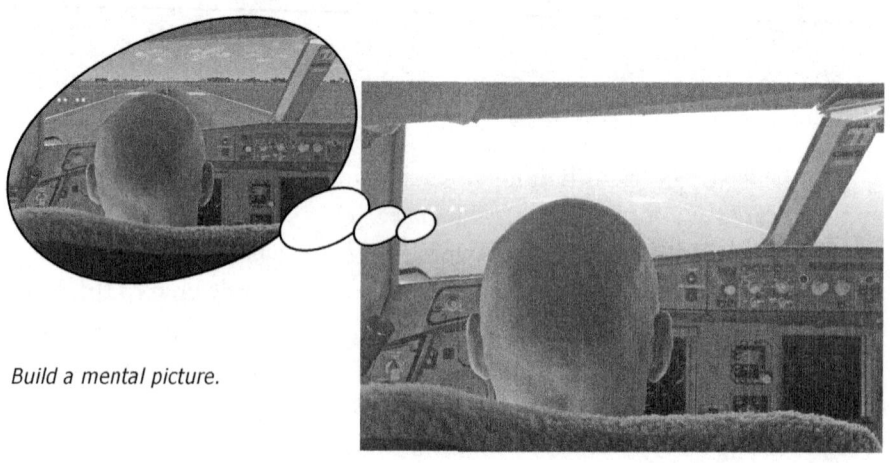

Build a mental picture.

the aircraft well. People always talk about the feedback a pilot gets through the "seat of their pants." Well, we don't know about you, but we have many more nerve endings in our heads than in our rear-ends! You receive more information through your vision than through any of the other senses (smell and taste have relatively little to do with flying; hearing does play a role, and feel is certainly important, but not as important as vision).

Much of the feel of flying comes from your vision. Imagine yourself looking just over the nose of the aircraft on take-off. If the aircraft begins to diverge off the centerline, you will be looking at a section of runway hardly displaced from the runway centerline at all. If you were looking farther ahead, almost to the horizon, the horizontal displacement of your sight from the centerline is much larger. In other words, the farther ahead you look, the more sensitive you will be to very slight changes in the direction of the aircraft.

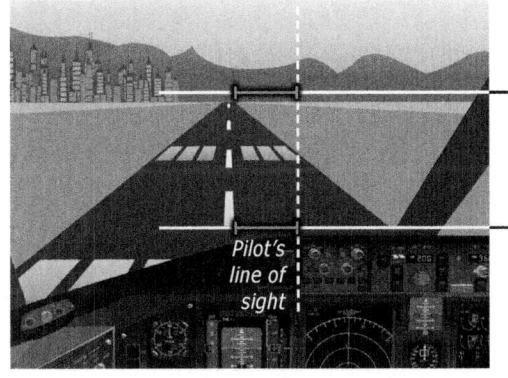

Directional change is more obvious when looking further ahead.

One of the most significant ways you can improve your visual input is to learn to juggle. Juggling for just five minutes a day can drastically improve your visual sampling rate, thinking speed, focus, and peripheral vision. Improved peripheral vision improves your ability to be attentive and alert by enhancing what you notice around you.

Unfortunately, peripheral vision deteriorates with age. Ever wondered why Grandpa is such a lousy driver? Left to its own devices, by the age of 80 your peripheral vision has roughly halved from

Improve your visual input through juggling.

its peak. The good news is peripheral vision is recoverable through training of the eyes and brain. Juggling is an excellent way to reverse the clock on peripheral vision by decades.

Let's just call it a bonus that on top of its benefits to visual input, juggling also acts as an excellent brain integration exercise!

Only the central few degrees of our visual field provides high-resolution vision. We subconsciously use rapid eye movements (saccades) several times per second to change our visual fixation point between points of interest and capture detailed snapshots that our brain then builds into a coherent understanding of our visual environment.

Consider that the serving speed of professional tennis players routinely exceeds 150 mph. At this speed, an opponent has only around 0.4 seconds before the ball arrives at their end of the court. Table tennis balls travel at only half that speed, but traverse the length of the table in less than 0.1 seconds!

To play successfully, in the time it takes for the ball to reach you, you've analyzed the body language of your opponent as they struck the ball. You've made an early assessment of the likely trajectory of the ball. You've visually acquired the ball and judged its trajectory and bounce. You've determined what stroke to play in return and moved into position to execute the required return.

Subsequently, tennis and table tennis are among the best forms of vision training available. By playing regularly, and ramping up the speed you play at, you will improve both your visual processing speed (i.e., the speed your brain processes information) and the amount of information your brain process from each saccadic snapshot.

Kinesthetic Input

If visual input and hand-eye coordination are associated, then kinesthetic input (or feel information) can be thought of as being associated with "hand-hand" coordination. Kinesthetic input is similar to visual (and auditory) input in that most of the information is constructed in your brain. If you were to practice feeling things with your hands over and over, do they become more sensitive? Yes and no. In actuality, your hands themselves do not become more sensitive, but your brain becomes better at constructing the feelings from the same amount of data sent to it. In the end, yes, you do become more sensitive, but because your brain (not your hands) has become more sensitive.

Ross had a dramatic demonstration of this fact while conducting a performance seminar for race car drivers. As part of a demonstration of the importance of sensory input, and for a little light-hearted fun, he asked two participants to compete in a race. Not a car race, though. The competition was to see who could pull on a pair of women's pantyhose in the least amount of time while blindfolded and wearing thick ski gloves. As you can imagine, with no visual input, and very little kinesthetic input, this was a real challenge (and resulted in more than a few laughs for the rest of the attendees).

Ross had become quite accustomed from previous seminars to how long it takes a person to complete the competition. In this one particular seminar, a participant completed it in less than half the time it normally takes. It seemed as though he was pulling on the pantyhose without the gloves. It wasn't until the end of the little race that they discovered he was a dental surgeon and worked all day long at very delicate maneuvers while wearing gloves, and not being able to see very well. To him, even through the thick ski gloves, he had some sensitivity. Through years of working with gloves and restricted visibility, he had developed that sensitivity.

If you were to practice flying wearing flying gloves (or thicker ones, if you already fly with gloves) and then switch back to no gloves (or your regular gloves), when it came time to perform (such as in a competition or on a check flight), your kinesthetic sensitivity would be enhanced. Therefore, your performance would improve.

As well as their hands, pilots also make significant use of their feet. Unfortunately, the kinesthetic feedback to our nervous system, along with the sense of position (proprioception), from our feet is much less precise than that from our hands and suffers greatly because of our wearing of footwear.

Our use of footwear and hosiery negatively affects the sensory nerve receptors that respond to pressure, touch, and movement.

Scientists believe that walking barefoot on irregular surfaces (such as rocks or cobblestones) for 20-30 minutes several times per week will improve your sensory input, balance, and proprioception. In fact, studies have shown that seniors engaged in regular walking programs on cobblestones showed significant improvement in blood pressure, mental health, mobility, and balance. Many cities, especially in China, are now installing pebble paths in parks for such reasons.

So, for deft manipulation of the rudder pedals and differential brakes, make a habit of ditching your shoes and socks! Besides, shoes are a new trend, having been around for only around five percent of the time humans have inhabited the earth.

The real point, again, is that your sensory input can be improved and developed; the further you develop your sensory input the greater sensitivity you will have to perform at your peak while controlling your aircraft. As we said in our Performance Tip, the key is to practice being aware. Many people go through life without really being aware of what is going on around them and what they can see, feel, hear, smell, and taste.

Auditory Input

In addition to hand-eye and "hand-hand" coordination, in reality, we also rely on "hand-ear" coordination where your brain processes information from your hearing and your body then performs the appropriate action.

An A320 captain friend of Phil's, who is also a competition aerobatic pilot, reports that he has very sensitive hearing. The downside for him is that he finds it hard to sleep with any noise present, but more interestingly, he finds he is quite attuned to the noises of the airplanes that he flies. He has noticed that some of the A320s in his airline's fleet make more noise than others and that he can tell when his Pitts Special is not flying "exactly right." While he has noted this can be disadvantageous if he lets little noise changes distract him, he is convinced that if used as an aid, he's able to tell if he is fast, slow, or has set the correct power setting.

Imagine flying with extremely effective earplugs; ones that block out almost all sound. You are moving the engine controls, changing your airspeed, deploying the spoilers, selecting gear and flaps, but you can barely hear any of the sounds normally associated with these activities. You strain to hear the engine; there is hardly any air noise at all. You have to rely more on the instruments than you have in a long time to determine whether you have made an appropriate thrust change or your airspeed is in the ballpark. There is auditory data going into your brain, just not as much as usual. You strain your hearing again to take in as much as possible.

If you have ever done a simulator session with the volume turned down or off, you will know this sensation entirely. It just feels different. It feels like you have to work harder to remain situationally aware. By the end of the session, you've got your flying rhythm back and you've learned to adapt to the lack of auditory input. The fact is, your brain is extremely adaptable and, in that short session, it had learned to perform nearly at the same level as it did before you restricted your auditory input. It has learned to be more sensitive. If you have access to a simulator and haven't tried this then why not do a session with the sound off to work on your other senses?

Alternatively, try flying while using earplugs (or heavier duty earplugs if you already wear them while flying) to restrict your auditory input. Then remove the earplugs (or go back to your regular ones) and notice how much more auditory input you receive. In single-pilot operations, or outside of a simulated flight environment, it may not be feasible or safe for you to try this exercise but if you can, the benefits are worthwhile.

Consider when you are back in the aircraft for a subsequent flight, but this time with your regular level of hearing protection. Now you have an abundance of auditory input. In fact, you may not have even realized how much sensory input you took in through your hearing before, but now you do. You are hearing the engine's throttle response like never before and are much more aware of the alteration in noise level with a change in your airspeed. You had never noticed all the sounds associated with the gear, flaps, and spoilers before. Wow! What a session! What a performance! You were magic in the aircraft. You were so much more aware. It was easy. That's what happens when you crank up the boost on just one of your sensory inputs.

Again, what you are doing is forcing your brain to work with restricted sensory input. Then, when it has gotten used to constructing the information with little data input, give back all the sensory input you can, when it counts.

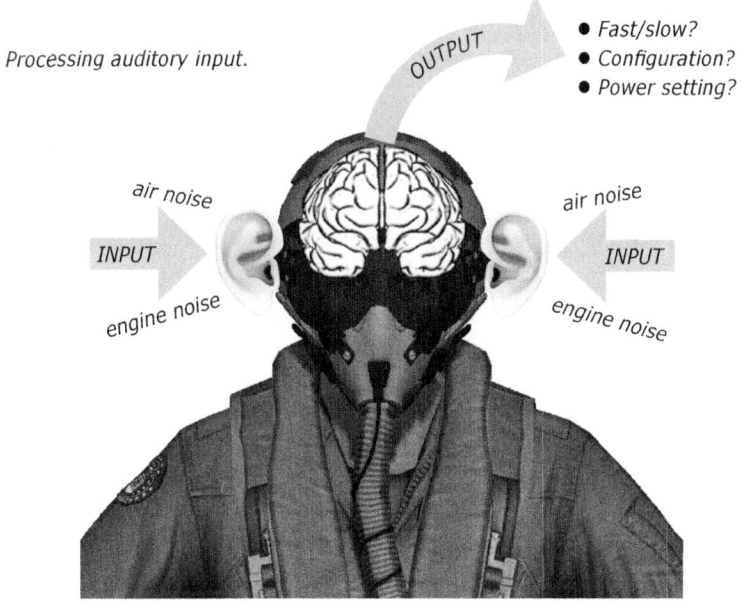

Errors and Sensory Input

Do you think experienced, exceptional pilots make any fewer errors than inexperienced pilots do? We don't think so. The only difference is the experienced pilot is better at minimizing the effects of them. They simply recognize errors earlier (due to taking in more sensory input) and react to them sooner and in a more subtle way. In other words, they minimize errors.

For example, when the experienced pilot makes an error such as flaring too early, they recognize it immediately and make small subtle corrections to either or both of their flare and thrust retardation rates - they make the best of the situation. When a less-experienced pilot makes the same error, they may not recognize it until they have floated deep into the runway or run out of airspeed and crunched it on.

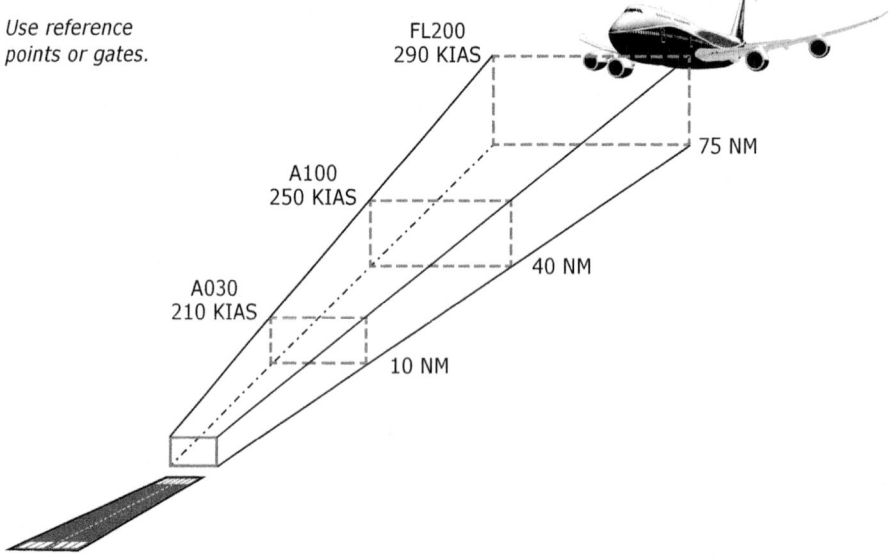

Use reference points or gates.

One way of reducing errors is by the use of reference points or gates. Gates are precise targets you have established for where you want to be in space and in what energy state: when, how high, how fast, what g, and in what configuration. The more reference points or gates you have for a sequence or a maneuver, the fewer errors you will make.

Most pilots have numerous reference power and attitude settings memorized for each phase of flight. Great pilots have dozens more of these reference points stored away subconsciously. To become a great pilot, you need to practice soaking up more information from your environment so that you see much more than just the basic reference attitudes for each phase of flight. You need an almost continual path of attitudes. These need to be in your mind at the subconscious level. That way, if you flare too late on landing, you recognize this instantly (at the subconscious level) rather than immediately before the main wheels impact the runway. The sooner you recognize it, the more subtle and effective the correction will be and the less negative impact it will have. At that level, you may not even notice the errors yourself; you seem to correct them before they even occur.

> **PERFORMANCE TIP**
> *The more reference points you have, the fewer errors you will make.*

But where and how does a pilot acquire more reference points? Is it only through more experience, more seat time? As a pilot gains experience, they usually get better at absorbing information to input into their computer - their brain - but this is a trend rather than a rule. Just because a pilot has lots of experience doesn't necessarily mean they have more reference points and therefore will be better at minimizing the effects of errors. Likewise, it doesn't necessarily mean that inexperienced pilots have fewer reference points.

A novice can be better at taking in information than other pilots who have been at it for twenty years. A pilot can also speed up the process by increasing the quality and quantity of sensory input. The more sensory information, the clearer the picture is of what's going on, and therefore, the better your reactions.

You can increase the quality and quantity of your sensory input by doing sensory input sessions. Of all the "tools" you can use to improve your flying performance, this is one of the most effective and yet most pilots have never done it. The ones who have often end up with a reputation for being very accurate, not making mistakes, and being great pilots because of their sensitive and accurate feedback on what the aircraft is doing.

> **PERFORMANCE TIP**
> *Minimize errors through maximizing sensory input.*

Sensory input sessions can reduce the number and extent of errors, both short-term and long-term, but how? Can you think of a pilot who has a reputation for making "bad decisions" in the aircraft? Often, the reason a pilot makes poor decisions or lacks awareness is that they lack the information upon which to base the decision. For some reason, the pilot making the error is missing some sensory input. It's like trying to make the decision to invest in a stock without having any past financial statements or annual reports.

Just like having more information about the financial performance of a company can help you make a better investment decision, the more information you have as you begin a sequence or maneuver, the better your decisions, physical actions, and corrections are going to be. In what attitude is the aircraft? Where around you is other traffic (friendlies or bogies) situated? What is the aircraft's energy state (airspeed and altitude)? How much g-force am I applying? What vibrations am I feeling? What can I hear from the engine and airflow?

Better information leads to better outcomes.

BETTER OUTCOMES

A lack of good information and a lack of quality sensory input may be the cause of many of the errors you make. If you are constantly landing beyond your desired touchdown zone, you and others may say you flared at the wrong height or rate. If you want to know the real reason why you're landing long, you have to dig to the core of the problem. You may know that you flared at the wrong height or rate but what is the reason, or cause, for you flaring where and how you did? What you saw as an adequate flare height or rate was not. Maybe you lack quality sensory input. You didn't have all the information, a complete picture. With more quality sensory input your decision-making will improve whether you currently make good decisions or not.

PERFORMANCE TIP
The better the information your senses provide to your brain, the more sensitive you'll be to what the aircraft is doing and what it needs.

Sensory Input Sessions

Sensory input sessions are a relatively simple way of improving the quality and quantity of sensory input you take in when flying. As we have stressed already, the better the quality and the more quantity of input from your senses that you can process, the better the quality of your performance.

First, go out for a flight, lesson, or simulator session with the sole objective of dedicating part of that flight or session to taking in extra sensory input. The best way of doing this is to determine how much time you have to do this exercise and then split that up over three flights or sessions. You should dedicate at least ten minutes, but not much more than fifteen, of each of the sessions to complete this exercise.

In the first session simply focus on everything you can hear. Focus on the engine note, the sound coming from the tires and brakes on landing, wind noise, and so on. Take in everything aurally - whatever you can hear.

For the second session, focus on kinesthetic input - everything you can feel. Notice any vibrations fed back from the flight controls through the control wheel or stick, rudder pedals, and seat. Note the amount the aircraft pitches, rolls and yaws, and how much lighter or heavier the control forces are as you change airspeed and g-load. If you are purposefully flying towards the aircraft limits, note any airframe vibration and the g-forces working against your body as you explore those limits.

The third session has you taking in everything visually. You should focus on what you can see - on being more visually aware of everything. Focus on discovering where the horizon cuts different parts of your visual field during different phases of flight and what you see on the horizon. Notice any vibrations and movements of the controls and other parts of the aircraft. Expand your view to take in more in your peripheral vision and see how the runway appears to bloom on very late final, expanding away from your aim point.

To make these sessions most effective, make notes on what you have discovered as soon as possible after each session. Sit and write down what you heard, felt, and saw at the end of the sessions. Ideally, describe to someone else what you heard, what you felt, and what you took in visually. Prod yourself for as much information and feedback as possible by asking yourself questions. In effect, debrief yourself on the exercise just as a flying instructor would for any sequence flown.

So, when should you use sensory input sessions? They are not a one-time deal and should be done regularly - especially after switching to a new aircraft or seat (congratulations, Captain!). The ultimate goal is to become more sensitive to all the sensory inputs. Sensory input sessions will help you familiarize yourself with an aircraft more quickly, become better at sensing when you're flying at the limit and provide you with much more feedback for developing your flying performance.

You may feel that you do not have time for these exercises – "I only have a finite amount of time in a flying lesson or simulator session, and I certainly don't want to waste that time just taking in sensory input!" Wrong! That is exactly the time to be focusing on sensory input. The goal is to learn as quickly as possible, and this is one of the best ways of doing that.

Sensory input sessions can also provide a "distraction" for your conscious mind; diverting your attention away from *trying* to fly better. Thinking too much, *trying* harder to fly better, never works. We have already established that the aviation environment is far too dynamic to operate aircraft proficiently at the conscious, trying level. We must fly them at the subconscious level with the conscious mind observing and being aware. What better distraction than having the conscious mind focused on providing the brain with more quality sensory input? If you can learn to recognize when you are trying too hard (and all pilots do at some time), you can use sensory input sessions to great effect.

Power + Attitude Sensing

One of the very first and most basic lessons you will have learned while learning to fly is that power plus attitude equals performance.

Just to ensure we are all on the same page, what we are saying here is that every combination of power setting (N1, EPR, RPM, RPM/torque, or RPM/MP) and attitude (bank angle and pitch) will equate to some level of performance. For example, in one of the light singles Phil instructed on, a power setting of 2,300 RPM and an attitude placing the horizon visually four finger widths above the glare shield would equate to flying straight and level at 110 KIAS (Knots Indicated Airspeed) at most cruise altitudes and weights. For an A330 in approach configuration, at a typical landing weight, if you set power at 57% N1 and the aircraft attitude at four degrees nose up you should be pretty close to the desired three-degree glideslope required for an ILS (Instrument Landing System) approach. No doubt you have, or should have, numerous combinations of power plus attitude combinations for your aircraft type to cover all phases of flight: take-off, climb, level off, turns, descent, traffic patterns, and the flare - all for different weights and configurations.

Power + Attitude = Performance.

As you become more experienced on the type (through muscle memory), you start to be able to accurately set power and attitudes with less reference to the instruments. Whereas you may have once relied on the gauges to set power and attitude, with familiarity you can do it instinctively, and accurately, with checks of the instruments becoming more for confirmation and fine-tuning. What if there was a quicker way to obtain this muscle memory? There is! In fact, there's more than one method! One is through the use of mental imagery (covered in a later chapter of this book), and the other is through power and attitude sensing exercises.

The aim here is to be able to set power and attitude very accurately without reference to your instruments. Most pilots develop this with time on type; however, there are a couple of exercises you can use to fine-tune your ability to do this. These exercises will enhance and expedite the process of developing this skill.

The first is done to develop your ability to estimate the power setting simply using sensory input without reference to the power gauges. While flying, every time you need to make a large power setting change for a change of phase of flight (e.g., cruise to climb or descent, entering a steep turn, setting up for an aerobatic maneuver), change the power setting with no reference to the engine instruments. Once you are satisfied that you have the thrust levers or throttles approximately where they should be, check to see how accurate you were. Correct any inaccuracy and then mentally note what the engine note sounds like with the power set accurately. How much did you have to move your hand to move the levers/throttle? With your hand on the levers/throttle, how does your new hand position feel in relationship to your body?

At the same time, when adjusting the attitude of the visual horizon for the new phase of flight, manipulate the controls to achieve the nose attitude and bank angle that you desire then check your attitude indicator to see how accurate you were. Adjust. Once you have the attitude set accurately, mentally note how much you had to manipulate the controls to reach the new attitude. Note also how your hand and arm position feel in relationship to your body. Where is the horizon cutting through various points in the windscreen? What can you see in your peripheral vision?

Horizon equidistant

Where does the horizon cut through the windscreen?

If you do these exercises over and over again you will become very accurate and, most importantly, consistent at judging and establishing desired power and attitude settings purely by engine note, visual reference, and muscle memory using sensory input as your guide.

Along similar lines, a practice of many of the pilots we spoke to in writing this book, is the deliberate practice of techniques that are supplementary or used less often. For example, once a month, or perhaps once per trip, the pilots we spoke to ensure they practice landing with manual thrust or using the flap setting they would use in wind shear conditions. Neither of these techniques is the normal procedure for the various models flown, but the pilots we interviewed were purposefully acquainting themselves with attitudes and power setting targets for the alternate configurations and, at the same time, developing muscle memories of the control inputs required. By deliberately practicing in benign conditions, our pilots were developing the sensory memories they would require to utilize these techniques in more challenging conditions successfully.

G-Awareness

If you are a fighter pilot or fly competition aerobatics, the ability to accurately sense and be aware of g-force is one of the key differences between a great pilot and all the rest.

To be able to fly at the limit of, but not beyond, the aircraft's capability without constant reference to the g-meter you must be able to feel or sense how much g-force you have applied. That sounds pretty obvious, but that is what g-awareness is: the ability to sense at any and all points of a maneuver exactly how much g-force you are applying or, put another way, it is the ability to sense if and when the aircraft is at the g-limit.

Of course, you could do this entirely by constant reference to the g-meter, but this decreases the amount of spare capacity you have to monitor other aspects of the maneuver you are completing or for general situational awareness. To establish yourself at the desired g-force entirely with reference to the g-meter would probably also extend the amount of time taken to reach the desired g-force. Knowing precisely when you are flying at the limit is, besides being the key to flying at the limit, an innate feel that one develops. We don't believe this is something that a person is either born with or not. Yes, some pilots seem to have a more natural feel or instinct for g-sensing, but any pilot who relies on accurately setting and holding a particular g-force can and must develop this feel and instinct.

Where does this ability to sense g-load application originate? It comes primarily from your senses and specifically your senses of feel, vision, and hearing. By simply being aware of the aircraft's g-load at all times, in all phases of flight, your g-sensing skills will improve. Also, there are a few specific exercises you can use to develop your g-awareness.

One of the things you can do while flying to enhance your g-awareness is simply to go out into the training area and apply g-force - in constant g-turns, in loops, or in any other maneuver you can hold the aircraft at the g-load you would like to be able to pull to accurately and hold. Start making mental notes once established in the maneuver. Do this by paying attention to the noise coming from the airframe, wind noise, and by the feeling through the controls. Notice how these factors change when going from straight and level into the maneuver. What are the sensations through your body? Note not just that your arms and head feel heavy, but how heavy. As you apply more g-force, do the control forces increase or do they decrease? Are they constant through the range of g-load and speeds? Does the aircraft give you any warning if you start applying excessive g-force? Is there buffet and, if so, how much? Practice calling out what g-load you think you are applying and then compare this to the actual g-meter reading. The more accurately you can describe your sensory inputs, the more accurately you will be able to recreate the maneuver relying solely on your senses.

"But I'm not a fighter pilot or involved in competitive flying. How does this relate to me?" Good question! For the vast majority of aviators, peak performance as a pilot requires we stay very far away from the edges of the performance envelope. In this instance, g-awareness comes into play when we are practicing steep turns. We may be practicing steep turns as a cross-reference exercise to build our skills or perhaps we are acquainting ourselves with what it feels like to be diverging from 1g flight so that we instinctively know to reduce the bank angle in an inadvertent spiral dive or reduce back pressure on the controls to avoid stalling.

> **PERFORMANCE TIP**
> *Use g-sensing sessions to improve your ability to fly at the appropriate g-load for the maneuver you're flying.*

The Federal Aviation Administration (FAA) (and most other civil aviation regulators) requires proficiency in steep turns as part of the Commercial Pilot Syllabus. So even if you are not flying to the full g-limit of your aircraft type, g-awareness exercises will be handy to become familiar with the 1.4g or 2g required to make level 45 or 60 degrees bank angle turns respectively.

If you use these techniques on a regular basis, we guarantee your g-awareness will improve, and that will lead to your ability to fly more consistently at the limit or an appropriate g-load.

Manipulation

As a further experiment, try holding the controls with your whole hand wrapped around the yoke or stick (so that your palm is fully in contact with the controls) in a tight grip. Notice the vibrations back through the controls. Next, hold the controls with just your fingers in a light, relaxed touch. Now notice the vibrations through the controls. Which provides the most feedback? In which way do you feel the most vibrations? Which allows you to make more subtle changes? You feel the most and fly more accurately with the light touch of the fingers on the controls, right?

Does this tell you something about how you should hold the controls? We hope so. If you consciously practice holding the controls with a light touch of your fingers, in all phases of flight, it will become a habit - a program. Yes, we know that some aircraft require more of a grip on the controls than what just your fingers can apply, but if you make a light touch a habit, you will apply the lightest touch possible on your aircraft controls. That will lead to increased sensitivity and therefore increased sensory perception abilities.

Don't choke the yoke! Tips are tops!

Protecting Our Senses

Having established the importance of the sensory information provided by the vestibular and auditory systems (affecting our senses of balance and hearing), and how we can improve this sensory information, it is worth noting what we can do to protect what we already possess.

A word of warning here; a serious one: flying an aircraft, or just hanging around the tarmac, without adequate hearing protection is a big mistake. In just a very short amount of time you can permanently damage your hearing. You should now know just how much your flying performance will be negatively affected if there is a reduction in your auditory input. So, before you get any ideas of heading out onto the tarmac with little or no hearing protection, don't!

As they age, or through exposure to a noisy work environment, many pilots begin to suffer from spatial hearing loss or spatial processing deficit. One of the ways this presents itself is the loss of the "cocktail party effect"; the ability to understand or focus on a single conversation in a noisy room in the presence of background noise.

Research indicates that it may be possible to train away some of this deficit. If you are having difficulty understanding chatter at a conversational level, practice watching television at a volume very slightly lower than what you usually do. With concentration, see if you can follow your programs as successfully as you had with the volume higher. If you can, then over time repeat the process and lower the volume again. Your end goal would be to be able to watch television at a normal, conversational level and hopefully restore some of the pre-training hearing deficit.

Upper respiratory tract infections (URTIs) can play havoc with our sense of balance. Not being able to achieve pressure equilibrium between our Eustachian tubes and ambient cockpit pressure stresses our eardrums and puts them at risk of rupturing. A ruptured eardrum has the potential to lead to a permanent hearing deficit. Therefore, for both immediate and ongoing peak performance flying considerations, it is of vital importance not to risk flying with a head cold.

Mental Programming

Neural Pathways

Imagine taking a cup of water and pouring it on top of a big mound of dirt and letting the water run down the hill. The first time you do this, the water will try to follow the path of least resistance and will begin to make a shallow pathway. The second time you pour a cup of water on top of the hill, it may follow the same path or it may find an easier, more natural, pathway. If it follows the same path, that pathway will become deeper and more ingrained. If it takes another path, it begins the path-building process all over again. Now, imagine pouring that same cup of water on the top of the hill a few thousand times a year for over twenty years. The pathway would be extremely well-routed, and it would be almost impossible for the water to follow any other pathway.

In much the same way, your brain starts to form neural pathways after doing something for the first time; they're there, but not very well established. The more you repeat an action, the more ingrained the neural pathways become.

Establishing neural pathways.

Every action you take in life is a result of your neural pathways (your mental programming). Consider the act of throwing a ball. At an early age, you probably observed someone throwing a ball. Then, maybe one of your parents tossed a ball to you and asked you to throw it back. Rather crudely, and without coordination, you managed to toss the ball in some direction. At that point, a neural pathway formed in your brain representing the physical act of throwing a ball. You threw the ball again, and the pathway became a little stronger. You threw again, and the pathway grew stronger yet again and so on. The first few times you threw the ball you had to think about how to do it consciously. At some point, when the neural programming became strong enough, you no longer had to think about it. Automatically, subconsciously, you ran the mental program and threw the ball.

The same is true of the techniques required to fly an aircraft. At first, while you are learning or programming an unfamiliar technique, you are consciously thinking about how to do it. Then, with repetition, your brain forms neural pathways or programs allowing you to sit on the flight deck or in the cockpit and simply execute the appropriate program at the appropriate time.

It's the same as going to the refrigerator for a drink. You don't have to consciously think to stand up, move your left leg in front of your right leg, the right leg in front of the left, and so on. You've done it so often; it's a subconscious act.

Flying Subconsciously

It is impossible to fly an aircraft accurately and efficiently at the conscious level. In other words, you cannot consciously think through the act of flying.

Aircraft are operated in a far too dynamic and complex environment to be able to do that, and there are just too many simultaneous hands and feet actions occurring and interacting with each other (remember flying lesson number one - primary and secondary effects of controls?). It has to be a subconscious act.

When we refer to pilots as being "naturals" we're referring to their ability to fly at the subconscious level. Like any skill, until the act of flying becomes a subconscious action part of your conscious mind will be used thinking about what you are doing rather than being aware of more important things. Remember the first time you drove a car? Steering, accelerating, braking, clutching, changing gears! How much of your brain capacity was available for anything else except thinking through these new physical skills?

To fly subconsciously you have to program your mind, but how do we do this? You program your mind by mentally and physically practicing. At first, it is a conscious act. For example, your conscious mind tells your feet to apply rudder as you change speed or thrust. After doing this over and over again it becomes programmed into your subconscious mind. Then, when required, it just happens automatically, without actually "thinking about it."

After thousands of repetitions of having their feet automatically apply rudder to counteract adverse aileron yaw when rolling into a turn, most pilots' neural pathways have a well-formed mental program for operating their feet when rolling into a turn. They then have to change that program when they first fly an aircraft with automatic rudder co-ordination. Instead of applying rudder while rolling into a turn, like they've always done before, they have to keep their feet neutral and only apply a roll input while letting the aircraft systems apply rudder.

Needless to say, when transitioning to heavy jets with automatic-rudder-coordination, many pilots with a background in propeller-powered training aircraft find it difficult not to apply rudder on take-off to counter the torque effect or when entering turns to allow for adverse aileron yaw. For good reason, right? After all, with that amount of repetition of applying coordinating rudder, that strong a mental program, that deep a neural pathway, it was almost as natural a movement as breathing.

Changing Programs

The good news is that for programs that are well-developed, you never have to give it even a fraction of a second of conscious thought. Programming leaves your conscious mind open to being used for more important things like monitoring traffic, listening to radio calls, cross checking of aircraft systems, or any of the other piloting duties that require conscious effort to accomplish. That is why it is so critical for the basic flying techniques to become habits - or mental programs - to allow your mind to concentrate on far more important things.

Now, the bad news. Any technique programmed into your brain can be difficult to change, as the pilots in our example discover when converting to their first type fitted with coordinated rudder. Do procedures change? Do flying conditions change, requiring different techniques? Do all aircraft react in the same way and require the same flying technique? The answers to these questions are, of course, "yes," "yes," and "no." You, therefore, have to be able to change or alter your mental programs quickly and efficiently.

More good news - your mental programming can be changed, but it does take some time. How do you do that? Firstly, you can achieve mental programming through actual physical practice. That's what stick time does; it develops the habits or programming to do things without having to think about them. When you fly at a subconscious level, it allows your conscious mind to "watch" what you are doing (seeing if there is anything you can do to improve technique-wise) or sense what the aircraft is doing handling-wise. As you fly subconsciously, by your "program," your conscious mind watches, senses, interprets what you and the aircraft are doing, and then makes changes to the "program" (subconscious) to improve. There is no point in continuously flying subconsciously if your "program" doesn't have you flying accurately or efficiently. Your conscious mind must always be working at reprogramming or updating your mind's "program," your subconscious.

However, there are a few problems with relying *only* on physical practice to build your mental programming:

- You'll spend a lot of money.
- You'll use (and maybe waste) a lot of time.
- You risk making mistakes part of your programming. Every time you make a mistake, you'll have made that mistake part of your mental programming. Practice does not make perfect; only perfect practice makes perfect. If you practice making mistakes, you'll only get better at making mistakes.
- You'll find it difficult to change your flying physically. If you're trying to do something that you've never done before, it can be almost

impossible to do it physically. As proof, have you ever known that a particular sequence can be flown (plenty of other pilots are flying it), but you just can't seem to get it together yourself no matter how hard you try and no matter how many times you tell yourself that you can do it?

- It can be risky. Experimenting with a new technique could lead to a miscalculation and result in an incident, or even worse, an accident!

Another method for changing your programming, and avoiding the pitfalls of relying *only* on physical practice, is through the use of mental imagery. Mental imagery is the deliberate use of what most people refer to as visualization. You may have also heard it referred to as "bedroom" or "armchair" flying. Why the distinction between visualization and mental imagery? Visualization, by the very definition of the word, uses only one sense (vision) in your imagined experience. As we will discuss in the next chapter, mental imagery involves more than just the sense of vision.

Using mental imagery to practice has many benefits and is very effective for numerous reasons:

> **PERFORMANCE TIP**
> *Practice doesn't make perfect; only perfect practice makes perfect.*

- It's perfectly safe. You can never hurt either the aircraft or yourself.

- You can mentally practice anywhere. You don't need an airport or an aircraft and, because of that, it's free. You don't need to sell this benefit to anyone paying for flying lessons by the hour!

- It may be the only place where you can fly a "perfect sequence." In your mind's eye, you can see yourself repeatedly flying exactly the way you want: the perfect altitude and speed, perfectly balanced, smoothly executing all maneuvers, and not missing any procedural items. When mentally flying an aircraft, perfection should be your aim. While learning to fly in the Royal Australian Air Force (RAAF), Phil spent many hours mentally rehearsing a particular electrical failure drill. When presented with this exact scenario in the aircraft, Phil diligently performed the task exactly as he had rehearsed it mentally - missing the same procedural item he had overlooked in his preparation! It's amazing how often an error in a pilot's mental imagery of a sequence happens, so visualize yourself doing it right!

- There's no fear of failure. You always fly perfectly, always as you wish. You can earn a perfect score on your initial license test, simulator check, or aerobatics routine, or win the air race or dogfight every time out if you wish.

- You can mentally practice in slow motion which gives you the time to be aware of each minute detail of the technique and perfect it before executing the sequence for real.

- You can mentally prepare for things that rarely occur in actual operations or that are open-ended scenarios. Student pilots can pre-rehearse engine failures after take-off (EFATO) or forced landings. Aerobatic pilots can string maneuvers together that may be part of the "unknown sequence." Fighter pilots can visualize dogfight scenarios, and commercial pilots can visualize complex failure scenarios. When you discuss "what if" scenarios with other pilots, you are helping each other mentally rehearse strategy and techniques. The result, when confronted with an abnormal situation, is that you are more prepared for it as you have practiced elements of scenarios so many times.

- Mental practice before actually flying forces you to automatically focus and concentrate.

Mental imagery is such a powerful tool that we are going to devote the entire next chapter to this one method of changing your mental programming.

Mental Imagery

There are many parallels to draw between flying and sport: passionate participants, considerable physical ability and skills involved, and competitive elements (air racers, aerobatics, aerial combat, or the driven student pilot aiming to best their previous efforts). Subsequently, there are many lessons pilots can take from the world of sport concerning preparation. Building a mental model, through mental imagery, is something that practically every superstar of every sport does. Do you want to be a superstar? Do you just want to improve your abilities and have more fun? Either way, mental imagery can provide you with a model of how to do things, when to do things, and even why to do things.

Your brain does not distinguish between real and imagined occurrences. Fortunately for you, it sees and accepts all images as if they were real. Therefore, it makes sense to "visualize," imagine or mentally practice flying.

Mental imagery is no stranger to aviation. Red Bull Air Race pilots set up drink cans to walk through a visual model of the track they will race. When given the sequence to be flown in a competition, aerobatic pilots draw the aerobatic box on the ground and walk through it over and over to learn the sequence. One of Phil's friends holds a pretend joystick and throttle as he walks through a sequence a few times before competing in his Pitts Special. Airlines and air forces all over the world provide their pilot trainees with cardboard cockpits and part-task-trainers so they can practice "touch drills." Fighter pilots use models on sticks to "see" different air combat scenarios unfolding.

> **PERFORMANCE TIP**
>
> *Fly in your mind before flying in the aircraft.*

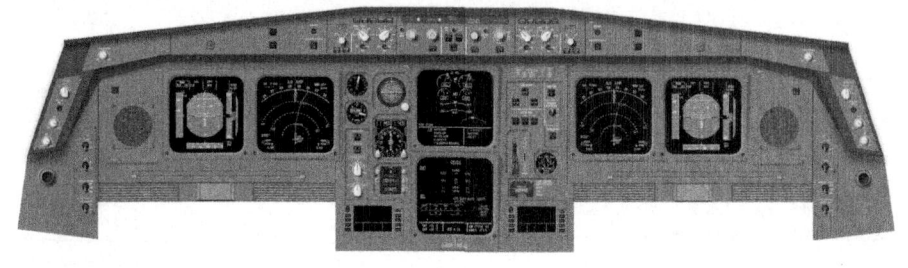

Front panel of an Airbus A330

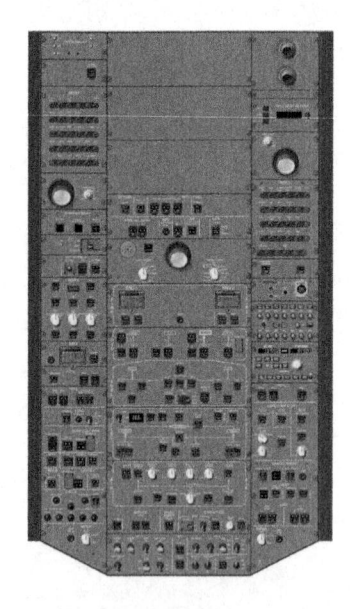

Left: Overhead panel of an Airbus A330

Right: Pedestal panel of an Airbus A330

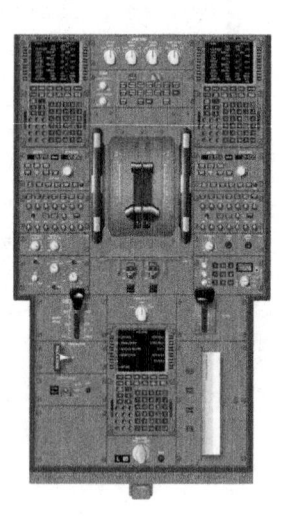

Effectiveness of Mental Imagery

But how effective is mental imagery compared to physically doing something? Of the many research studies and examples of the impact of mental imagery, here are three:

- **Hunter College basketball players study:** A group of basketball players was asked to shoot free-throws, and the success percentage was measured. The players then split into three separate groups. The first group was told not to practice whatsoever, physically or mentally. The second group was asked to practice daily by actually shooting free-throws. The third group was asked only to do mental imagery of shooting perfect free-throws each day and not physically touch a basketball. When checking the players' free-throw percentage a week later, the results were interesting. Unsurprisingly, the first "no practice" group showed no improvement whatsoever. The second group, the ones that had physically practiced each and every day shooting free-throws, improved their shooting accuracy 23%. The last group, the ones that only did mental imagery each day and did not touch a basketball? Well, they improved their free-throw shooting percentage 22%. Without touching a basketball, they improved 22%, essentially the same amount as the group that physically practiced each day.

- **Soviet Union Olympic study:** During the 1980s, what was then the Soviet Union's Olympic team tested various training procedures. Athletes from various sports split into four groups. The first group trained entirely with physical practice, 100% of the time. The second group used physical training 75% of the time and mental imagery 25% of the time. The third group split its training 50-50, and the fourth group spent 25% of the time training physically and 75% of the time mentally. The mental training required them to spend time every day practicing their sport in their minds using mental imagery. At the end of the study, the group who had made the biggest gains or improvement was the fourth group, the one that had spent only 25% of the time training physically and 75% of the time using mental imagery. It's interesting that the group which trained 100% of the time physically actually improved the least amount.

- **American Prisoner of War**: While this is not a formal research study, the following true story provides a great example of the power of mental imagery. An American prisoner of war was held captive for five years. Before the war, golf had been his passion, his favorite pastime. During the time he was held captive, he mentally played a couple of rounds of golf every single day, and he played them perfectly. He saw the green of the grass and the shots he hit. He felt his swing, the connection with the ball, and he even felt the way the grass felt underneath his shoes as he walked the course. He heard the sounds of the birds in the trees, the wind, the sound of his club hitting the ball and it soaring down the fairways. He imagined every last detail of how his perfect round of golf would look, feel, and sound. When released from prison one of the first things he did was hit the links. Despite not having touched an actual golf club in over five years, and only having played golf mentally through that time, he shot the very best round of golf he ever had.

As an example of the power of mental imagery you can do immediately, try this. Read the following italicized narrative at least three times. After you've read it, close your eyes, breathe deeply and slowly, relax, and then imagine the scenario that you've just read. Try to imagine as many of the details that you read as you can. See, feel, hear, smell, and taste the scenario.

"To begin, make yourself comfortable, with your hands resting in front of you. Close your eyes. Breathe deeply, taking nice, slow breaths. Relax your body. Allow your muscles to relax. Feel your body sink into the chair. Feel your body get heavy and relaxed. Hear your heartbeat slow down. Continue to breathe slowly and deeply. If you should feel yourself start to drift off to sleep, just take two or three quick, deep breaths, and that will bring you back to a relaxed, but awake state. Breathe slowly. Relax your muscles.

"Breathe. Relax.

"Imagine a bright yellow lemon sitting on a table in front of you - a bright, shiny, yellow lemon.

"Now, imagine picking that bright yellow lemon up with both hands. Feel the texture of the skin and shape of the lemon. Notice how bright the yellow is.

"Imagine placing the lemon back on the table in front of you. There is a knife sitting on the table. Pick it up. Place the blade on the lemon and slice it in half, hearing the sound of the blade slicing through the lemon.

"Notice the juices dripping onto the table. See the lemon juice on the blade of the knife. See the lemon in two halves with juice on the table around it.

"Pick up one-half of the lemon and give it a squeeze. As you feel the lemon squashing, notice the juices on the face of the lemon dripping back onto the table.

"Bring it up to your nose and smell the lemon. Breathe deeply as you smell the scent of the lemon.

"Now, bring the lemon to your mouth, stick out your tongue, and slowly lick the juices off the face of the lemon. Taste the juice.

"Continue to taste the lemon juice in your mouth.

"Okay. When you're comfortable, slowly open your eyes as you mentally come back into the room."

"See the lemon, feel the lemon, smell the lemon, taste the lemon..."

What happened? What did you experience? Did your mouth pucker up? Did you have saliva build up in your mouth? Yes? If you're like most people, your mouth began to salivate. Why? Your brain is unable to tell the difference between a real and an imagined event. Because your brain thought there was real lemon juice coming into your mouth, your brain triggered saliva to water down the citric acid of the lemon.

This exercise is a simple example of the power of mental imagery. It's why superstar athletes, and, in fact, anyone who depends on performing at a high level, use it. It's why, if you want to make a change in your behavior or improve or develop a skill, using mental imagery is a critical step - perhaps the most important.

Uses of Mental Imagery

For many pilots, the use of mental imagery is limited to familiarizing themselves with a sequence or for pre-practicing a specific technique before sitting behind the controls. For these pilots, they are missing out on some of mental imagery's best uses. Overall, you can and should use mental imagery for all of the following:

- **To see success:** You can develop your belief system by recalling past success and pre-playing success in future events. Your belief in your abilities may be the most important key to success, more important than natural or developed skill, and you can improve it with mental imagery. We will discuss belief systems in a later chapter.

- **To motivate:** By recalling the emotional feelings of past successes, and imagining them for future events, you can remind yourself of what you enjoy most about flying. When things are not going well (as they often do for every pilot at some point in their flying career), focusing on what you truly get out of flying can lead to superior performance.

- **To trigger a performance state of mind:** By vividly recalling your feelings of a past success, it's almost impossible not to get into a great state of mind. Over time, and by building in a "trigger," you can simply say a word or perform an action to get into the ideal state to perform at your peak.

- **To program behavior:** You need to behave in different ways in different situations. By pre-playing these situations and adapting your behavior, you improve your ability to act in an ideal manner (e.g., more assertively, more patiently, or in a more out-going manner) when the need arises. Mental imagery programs the ability to adapt your behavior to suit the situation.

- **To pre-plan:** Although there are an infinite number of possibilities that can happen in flight, pre-planning for as many of them as possible will allow you to act more quickly, more accurately, more confidently, and with more ease. For example, pre-playing some non-normal or emergency scenarios that could occur during a flight will help you develop the attitude that "it doesn't matter what happens; I'm ready."

- **To re-focus**: If you form a mental image of yourself dealing with problems in the air, especially the problem of losing your concentration and then immediately re-focusing and continuing, you will develop a program for doing this. When it happens in the air, it will be much easier to regain your focus.

Types of Mental Imagery Sessions

Sports psychologists define two different types of mental imagery: cognitive (technique-specific) and motivational (relaxed, balanced, confident, enjoyment-specific). These two types are further broken down into general and specific subtypes. You should balance your mental imagery sessions between each of the four resulting subgroups. To give you an idea of how you would use each type of mental imagery, consider the following:

- **Cognitive Specific:** Forming mental imagery for the rehearsal of specific skills, e.g., V1 cuts, engine fires, go-arounds, traffic patterns, instrument approaches, etc.

- **Cognitive General:** Forming mental imagery for the rehearsal of strategies, e.g., establishing the "aviate, navigate, communicate" protocol as a generic sequence for handling abnormal situations.

- **Motivational Specific:** Goals and goal attainment, e.g., setting mental objectives and goals for a flight and having these objectives and goals be more than just something you've thought about at the conscious level; they've become a part of your mental programming.

- **Motivational General**: Arousal control, self-confidence, mental toughness, e.g., where you develop mental programming of your beliefs, confidence, state of mind, behavioral traits, overcoming pre-test nerves, not giving up, control or use of emotions, and the "rewards" of a job well done.

Mental imagery can also be "associated" or "dissociated." Associated means you see, feel, and hear yourself in the very act. That is, you're behind the controls, and your view is from this vantage point. Dissociated is as if you see yourself from above or from a camera view and not from behind the controls. For some reason, some people naturally do mental imagery from an associated perspective while others do it from a dissociated perspective.

Associated vs dissociated mental imagery.

So, which is best, associated or dissociated? Some people will tell you that neither one is better than the other; however, we disagree. Doing some mental imagery from a dissociated perspective (watching yourself perform from an instructor's viewpoint) is valuable, but it's best to program your mind from the perspective you'll experience when flying - behind the controls.

The key is to make your mental imagery as real as possible by seeing the view from the cockpit, by feeling the aircraft and motions from the seat and hearing everything from behind the controls. A message you'll hear over and over from us is that the more realistic you can make your mental imagery, the more effective this whole process will be.

Getting Started

Many people will ask, "But if I've never done it before, how can I even imagine doing it, much less create mental imagery of it?" That's a very good point. Without some idea of what "doing it" looks, feels, and sounds like, it's hard to imagine it.

There's no point in mentally flying an aircraft or sequence you've never actually seen before without some reference. Without some prior knowledge, some background information, you may just be practicing something the wrong way. Visualizing an error is practicing an error. Practicing an error is a sure way of ensuring you will repeat it.

The good thing is that, even if we haven't seen a sequence before, we do have a starting point. Flight Crew Operating Manuals (FCOM), Flight Crew Training Manuals (FCTM), coordinated briefings, instructor briefs, etc. give us the basics of the sequence of events for the maneuver to we want to fly, the location of controls, flows for switching, attitudes, and speeds to fly. Briefs from instructors will often include actual photographs or diagrams on the desired sight picture at each stage of the maneuvers we are going to fly. As examples, where the horizon should appear for straight and level or other phases of flight, the position of the runway relative to the wingtip on the downwind leg or base turn point in the traffic pattern, visual references for flying in formation. Once we have flown a sequence in real time, either in the air or the simulator, we can return to mental programming to reinforce our performance for the future.

Writing a Narrative

Before beginning a mental imagery session, you should know precisely what you want to accomplish. To set out what you want to accomplish, you could write a narrative much like the one for the lemon example we introduced earlier. The reason for writing out a plan for your narrative is to make sure you stay on task. By doing this before beginning, it's more likely that you will stay focused throughout the imagery session. By that, we mean staying focused on what you're working on: working on a specific sequence or technique, dealing with abnormal and emergency situations, being the perfect pilot, flying at the limit, or whatever.

You can make your narrative extremely detailed, or you can make a few short bullet points to help you remember the key points you want to program. In an interview in *Flight Safety Australia* magazine, Red Bull Air Race pilot, Matt Hall talked about the strategies he has used throughout his career as a fighter combat instructor and air racer. There can be no doubt that Matt is a peak-performance pilot. Matt described how his mental preparation for a race involves writing out a highly structured, comprehensive, second-by-second script for the flight he is about to complete. Matt estimated that he would write around ten pages of notes for a seven or eight-minute flight. The sort of information he includes are the energy states he's looking for, the g-load he'll use, where he will be looking, how aggressively he will fly, and what the control forces will be. He then learns his script, mentally flying the script in slow time and working his way up to real time.

When you're ready to begin a mental imagery session, read the narrative that you've prepared. If you don't have your narrative firmly in your mind, you risk straying away from what you've outlined and not being able to replicate it once your mental imagery session begins. The only way for this programming to be truly effective is to repeat it enough times to form new (or reinforce existing) neural pathways. Repetition is critical.

The Right State of Mind

After you've read through the narrative and you've got it memorized well enough to be able to follow it over and over again for 20 minutes, what then is the right or ideal mental state to be in to program your mind? Let's start with a little background theory. Doctors and researchers define four brainwave states as measured by an electroencephalograph (EEG). By attaching a few probes to your head, the EEG can "read" the bio-electrical activity going on inside your head and therefore measure the brainwaves. These brainwaves are broken down into four levels or states:

- **Beta,** where your brain is primarily producing brainwaves in the 13 to 25 Hz (cycles per second) range. When you're in a conscious, thinking, active state, like when you're reading this book, your mind is in the Beta range.

- **Alpha**, where your brain is primarily producing brainwaves in the 7 to 13 Hz range. Alpha is when you close your eyes, relax and begin slowing down your mind. While getting to this state, you should feel your body relax, your muscles letting go and your body sinking into your chair or seat.
- **Theta,** where your brain is primarily producing brainwaves in the 4 to 7 Hz range. Just before you fall asleep, you pass through a state where you can feel yourself drifting off, but you're barely aware that you're doing this. You may also have flashes of odd images in your mind.
- **Delta,** where your brain is primarily producing brainwaves in the 0 to 4 Hz range. When you're asleep, your mind is producing mostly Delta waves.

Notice that we never said that your brain is only producing one level of brainwaves at a time. No, it's always producing some amount of all four but, depending on what state you're in, the concentration of the various levels changes. When consciously awake, conversing, thinking, reading, and flying an aircraft, your mind is producing mostly Beta waves, some amount less of Alpha, less Theta, and much less Delta. When asleep you're mostly producing Delta, less Theta, less Alpha, and even less Beta.

So, what does this all mean?

For your brain to be in the most receptive and effective programming state you want to relax your mind enough so that it is in what is called an Alpha-Theta state. In this state of mind, your brain is primarily producing brainwaves in the 6 to 12 Hz range. The best way to describe this state is that your mind is not busy, it's relaxed. You haven't drifted off to sleep yet but if you let your mind relax and slow down much more you would.

If you simply close your eyes and consciously think about something your mind will be in a Beta state and the effectiveness of your mental imagery will be significantly reduced. Herein lies a major and common misconception. Thinking about flying the aircraft is *not* mental programming, and it's *not* mental imagery. Thinking about something is done at the conscious level, and the conscious level is not the most effective state of mind to be in to learn something effectively and for it to become part of your mental programming.

Until you allow your brain to get into the right mental state, you're not using mental imagery to program your subconscious. By allowing yourself to get to an Alpha-Theta state, by relaxing your mind and body, everything that you imagine will become imprinted within your brain much more deeply and strongly and this is how you program your mind. From there your ability to reproduce it in the air is much greater.

Of course, getting your mind into an Alpha-Theta state at home, lying on your bed, is relatively easy. Getting there while in a part-task trainer or sitting in your aircraft in the hangar is more difficult. Why? It's because of the distractions and the possible stress in these environments. Fortunately, like most things in life, the more you practice, the easier it will get.

To get into an Alpha-Theta state where your mind is slowed down and very receptive, get yourself in position, close your eyes and breathe deeply and slowly three or four times. Relax. Starting at your toes and working towards your head, feel each part of your body relaxing. Feel yourself relaxing. Feel your muscles begin to let go. Feel yourself begin to sink into your chair or seat. Listen to your heartbeat slow down. Notice your breathing slow down as you become even more relaxed. Notice the images of yourself as a relaxed person sinking into your chair or seat. Breathe. Relax your muscles. Breathe. Count your breaths. As you do each of your imagery sessions, continue to breathe and be relaxed. Part of what you're programming is the ability to feel relaxed and breathe normally throughout these scenarios. Breathe. Relax. You're now ready to begin the mental imagery session from your narrative.

With practice, you will know when your mind is slowed enough and is in an Alpha-Theta state. You may notice some odd and unrelated images flashing through your mind. It's near that stage, just before you fall asleep but still awake enough to be aware of what's going on around you, that your mind will be in a receptive state for mental programming. It can take anywhere from two to five minutes to get to this state (it will probably take less and less time with practice). If you find yourself falling asleep, take three or four quick breaths to produce an increase in Beta waves.

As an aid to getting into an Alpha-Theta state, you may like to consider using pre-recorded music tracks used for self-hypnosis. You can use these tracks in the relaxation stage of your mental imagery sessions.

Triggers

Mental imagery is an extremely powerful technique that results in the development of mental programs. These mental programs allow you to do things without "consciously thinking" about them. You do them "automatically," by habit.

Just as you have a mental program for walking, and therefore do not have to think about how to walk, you can develop a mental program for the act of flying an aircraft and then rely on that program to fly the aircraft. In fact, that's the goal - to get to the point where the act of flying or being a pilot is a program, where you no longer have to think about what you need to do consciously, you just do it.

The reason you "just do it" is because you've developed a mental program that resides in your subconscious and you've triggered or launched it. Just like launching a software program on your computer, you can launch or "trigger" a mental program when you need it.

Now, imagine installing the latest, most powerful software package into your computer but it not having an icon on the desktop or start menu to access it. Imagine the frustration! How useful would a computer program be without an icon or trigger to launch it? It wouldn't be very useful at all, right?

The same thing applies to a mental program. Imagine if you did mental imagery over and over again and developed the programming to fly the one sequence or maneuver you've never been able to perfect before, such as a complex recall or phase one checklist. You can see, feel and hear it so clearly in your head. Then, in the simulator or (even worse) when you experience an actual failure, you can't locate that mental program in the vast hard drive in your head. Imagine the frustration!

That is what it would be like if you had the ideal program for flying but not a "trigger." Triggers are actions and words that allow you to access or activate a mental program. You could have all the mental programming in the world, but without a trigger, you will never activate it. So, as important as mental imagery is, it's just as important to develop a trigger to launch this program. A trigger word or action works just like a gun's trigger. Trigger words or actions should have some special meaning or generate a vivid mental image.

The coach of Olympian Michael Phelps tells him to "put in the tape" when he wants Michael to commence mental imagery of swimming perfectly and dealing with a variety of possibilities that could occur during a race.

As an example, to trigger a program to soak up sensory input you might use the word "sponge" to see yourself as a sponge soaking up all there is to know. Other examples could be "go-around," "reject," "wind shear," "engine fire," "TCAS," "snap roll," and "relax." Trigger actions could include giving the controls a quick squeeze, looking at a specific sign or message on the panel, or a hand signal from your ground crew.

You may need to spend some time discovering just the right words, phrases, or actions to use as triggers.

When you are using mental imagery to create programs, initiate them with your specific trigger words or actions in your mind as you imagine working through the associated sequences over and over again. The more you do this, the more your mind will associate the triggers with the associated programs. Eventually, you'll get to the point where, when you are in the heat of the battle, the second you say your trigger words, or use your trigger actions, the programs will kick in. It's just like the renowned dog from the famous experiments by Ivan Pavlov.

Sensory Immersion

The more senses you include in your mental imagery, the more effective it will be. Notice in the lemon example that you used all five senses. You "saw" the lemon (visual), you "felt" the lemon (kinesthetic), you "heard" the knife cutting the lemon (auditory), you "smelled" the lemon juice (olfactory), and you "tasted" the lemon (taste). But in actuality did you see, feel, hear, smell, and taste the lemon? Yes, but only in your mind, right? Yes, only in your imagination. By involving all five senses, you made the experience very real in your imagination. If you had only "seen" the lemon, using only your visual sense, it's likely that your mouth would not have salivated because you would not have made it real enough to your mind.

Obviously, your smell and taste have relatively little to do with flying an aircraft but certainly visual, kinesthetic, and auditory senses have a lot to do with it. Most people who claim to do mental imagery in actuality are only visualizing. That is, they only imagine the visual scene in their minds; they do not imagine what they feel and hear. That's the difference between mental imagery and visualization - mental imagery involves more than just your visual sense and visualization doesn't.

Mental imagery session in progress.

We need to stress again that the more senses you involve in mental imagery, the more effective the programming will be. Use your hands; hold the control column or stick (even if it's an imaginary one). Move your feet; feel the rudder pedals. Hear the engine, the wind noise, the gear, flaps, and speed brakes actuating.

By sitting at a cardboard cut-out representation of the cockpit, or in a part-task trainer, pilots can short-cut some of the imagination elements using actual visual images. Along the same lines, "walking through" an aerobatic maneuver by turning in the direction he was going to be looking in the cockpit helped a friend of Phil's when he was learning to fly barrel rolls. Most of the student pilots on Phil's military pilots' course used this same method to "walk through" traffic patterns and forced landing procedures.

Part-task trainer.

Remember, the more you use your body, the more the session will program muscle memory to do things right when you're flying. If you don't use your aircraft, use as many "props" as you can to make it as realistic as possible. You can wear your helmet or headset, and you can hold a real control column or something to simulate it. You can ask someone to sit on the floor in front of you and use their feet as rudder pedals. Using a partner's feet as rudder pedals is a very effective technique as you can even have them provide feedback to you on the amount of pressure you're applying and the progressiveness of the application. Sitting in a flight simulator is fantastic since you can begin by flying a sequence and then go into your mental imagery session. Of course, you have a yoke or stick and pedals to use with a simulator as well. Again, the more realistic you can make your imagery session, the more effective it will be.

In addition to your visual, kinesthetic, and auditory senses, experience all the emotions and feelings that you possibly can. The more you tie your emotions and feelings to each mental imagery session the more real it will become to your mind. More importantly, the easier it will be to trigger the specific mental program in the future. This motivational piece of mental imagery is critical to your success.

Staying Focused During a Session

Many pilots talk about not being able to stay focused on the specific scenario that they want to imagine and program for very long. Some pilots have a difficult time doing a specific mental imagery scenario for much longer than a minute or two. If that's how it feels to you, know that you're human. In his work as a performance coach, everyone Ross has ever talked to about mental imagery admits that they have trouble focusing. Those that continued to practice mental imagery get better and better to the point where they may be able to stay focused on imagining a scenario for up to an hour or even more. Those who get frustrated that they can't do it perfectly the first time tend to quit and, of course, never improve.

If it helps you when you are beginning to use mental imagery, you can record your narratives on a voice recorder and play them back as a form of guided mental imagery. One method Phil has seen used by trainee pilots is to write a bullet-point list of sequences they want to fly. The trainee gives the list to a facilitator who sits with the trainee. As the trainee raises a finger to indicate they have completed mental imagery of an event in the list, the facilitator verbally prompts the next item in the list. Both of these methods ensure that, during the initial stages of a new mental imagery session, the trainee follows the narrative perfectly, doesn't miss anything, and the session remains focused which helps the trainee avoid having their mind wander.

Emerson Fittipaldi, former Formula One and Indy Car driver, won the Indianapolis 500 in 1993. The day before the race he spent over three hours sitting in his car in the garage. He claimed that if he couldn't imagine sitting in the car for that long, there was no way he was going to be able to drive the entire race without losing his focus.

Optimizing Your Sessions

Mental imagery is an acquired skill, so don't expect instant results. As with any other skill, with patience and practice your ability to use it will improve.

If you are serious about your flying, you should do at least two sessions a day, seven days a week. It's best to perform mental imagery once in the morning and once at night, and for a minimum of 20 minutes. You can take a day off if you want, but if you're involved in some form of competitive flying you can bet some of your competitors won't. If you take a day off, they are getting an advantage on you. You can split the sessions over the day, any way that suits your lifestyle, but there should be at least one hour between the two sessions.

Also, have a plan for the type of skill or technique you're going to practice. Mondays could be for programming specific flying skills, Tuesdays for working on your beliefs about your abilities, Wednesdays for competition strategy, Thursdays for your overall state of mind, and so on.

Even when pre-playing a success to develop your confidence or motivation, focus your mental imagery on the act or performance. Sure, see yourself be successful but focus on what led to the success: the way you felt, the way you performed, the state of mind you were in, and the actual skills and techniques it took to get there.

You should also determine a consistent place to practice mental imagery. Preferably, this is not lying on your bed as there is too much of a tendency to fall asleep while doing it. Sitting in a chair is good and in your aircraft or a part-task trainer is even better. You want to make sure you are comfortable and relaxed, that it's quiet, and you will not be disturbed.

One last point about mental imagery: don't expect it to compensate for lack of knowledge, hard work, or practice. While it can and will make a huge difference to your performance, it can't perform miracles.

Computer Simulation

Consider the amount of money airlines and air forces of the world spend on expensive, realistic, full-motion simulators. With the cost of computer hardware coming down all the time, even local flying schools are starting to install some reasonably complex and realistic fixed-base simulators. So what about home simulators for personal computers? Can they play a role in you becoming a better pilot? The answer is, "yes." As personal computer based flight simulations become more and more realistic, they can act as an excellent, inexpensive procedure and task training aid in addition to being a very useful adjunct to mental imagery.

These simulations can be valuable in helping a pilot develop a virtual reality visualization, although there are a couple of limitations. First, of the three sensory inputs a pilot relies on (visual, auditory and kinesthetic), simulations do a good job with two (visual and auditory) and a very limited, if any, job of the third (kinesthetic). Second, how much does flying a Boeing

737 out of JFK help a Cirrus SR22 pilot preparing for a flight out of their local airport? Mental rehearsal of flying one type of aircraft does not necessarily apply to another, but this is not an issue if you can purchase a detailed add-on for the aircraft type you fly.

If you have a detailed add-on for the actual aircraft you will be flying then a home-based simulator will allow you to familiarize yourself with the functions and use of its various systems, instruments, and controls without needing access to the actual aircraft. You may also be able to practice partial panel instrument flying, various failure scenarios that aren't able to be realistically replicated on a normal flight, or play out complex "what-if" scenarios.

Having said that, even if you can't get an add-on for your type, or the add-on is less than a 100% accurate representation, there are things that a "sim pilot" can practice that will help once in the air. You can practice the ability to focus concentration for longer periods. You can also develop a fine sensitivity manipulating the control column or stick. Finally, you can practice learning. It doesn't matter whether you are flying an F-35 Lightning II, Edge 540, Cirrus SR22, Airbus A380, or a computer simulation. The process of determining what works, what doesn't, what effect a change in technique has, or whether a change is necessary is one of the things that separates the great pilots from the rest.

A pilot must be able to adapt their personality/behavioral traits to suit various situations, to control and trigger the ideal state of mind, and make quick, appropriate decisions. If correctly used, a flight simulation can certainly help a pilot mentally program and develop these abilities.

There is much more to flying than just the basic motor skills. A good simulator will allow you to put into practice many of the procedural items that go beyond the basic motor skills required. Before you even get to the airport for a lesson, you can use a simulator for:

- practicing running checklists,
- familiarizing yourself with a new destination,
- changing weather parameters to see what you will be able to see when breaking visual at various minima on instrument approaches,
- practicing allowing for the effects of varying wind components, or
- route preparation for navigation exercises if your simulator has a good visual model (available for some areas as a purchasable add-on).

Pilots training for an instrument rating can use pretty much any simulator to build their scan rate using cross-reference exercises, improve their ability to ascertain their position and build situational awareness using only navigation aids, practice sector entries and holding patterns, or fly precision approaches. Even if you have had an instrument rating for more renewals than you can remember, a simulator is a fantastic training and proficiency tool as it allows you to maintain your scan and embed the procedural elements of instrument approaches.

If you are having difficulty mastering a particular part of your flying, many simulators allow you to isolate tasks and divide complicated procedures into subparts by allowing you to pre-set your starting position. You can (for example) place yourself on final to practice landings or at the beginning of an instrument approach. In this way, you can dispense with pre-flight checks, taxiing, take-off, climbing, transits, etc. and, instead, dedicate your valuable practice time to just the elements that need the most attention. Simulators also allow you to invest all your concentration on the task at hand without the distractions of real world flying such as dealing with other traffic, but that being said that, if desired some simulators even have the ability to add a traffic element.

At the end of each sequence flown, home simulators will usually allow you to replay flights using data captured while you were flying. You can use a replay to help debrief either by yourself or with an instructor in much the same way as fighter pilots review head up display (HUD) tapes or naval carrier pilots review their landings. Looking at a map overlay view of your flight, you can assess how accurately you've flown a traffic pattern, sector entry, holding pattern, or tracked the localizer and glideslope on an ILS.

Overall, simulation is another tool that pilots can and should use to develop and maximize their performance. Just as only using physical practice, simply studying manuals, or relying solely on mental imagery will limit your ability to learn, only using simulations will not result in you becoming the next "ace from space." A simulator is not a substitute for time in the air but, combined with all the other tools a pilot has available, simulations are very valuable.

Learning

If you had to choose just one thing that separated the real superstars of any pursuit from the rest, what would it be? Superior hand-eye coordination. The desire to succeed? Work ethic? Natural talent? While all of these traits, and many others, are factors, the one thing that truly separates the greats from the not-so-greats is the ability to learn. In our opinion, the peak performers in any activity are not necessarily born with any more natural talent than anyone else. It is what they do with that natural talent that makes them great.

Rather than just assuming that you have only so much talent in your mind/body, why not learn more, why not develop your talents? This chapter is all about how we learn and presents a powerful strategy you can use for learning that builds on our discussion on mental imagery.

Learning as an Objective

If you want to be a great pilot, every time you get airborne there is one single most important objective that will ultimately lead to achieving all other objectives. That objective is to learn. To perfect your flying, you should constantly be striving to learn more and improve your flying and fly more smoothly. Keep your mind open to new techniques.

Learning to fly is one of the most enjoyable challenges in the world. If you continue to learn, becoming a more capable, more proficient pilot will come naturally. When you learn, you will continue to improve your performance. By improving your performance, you increase the chances of achieving the results you desire from your flying.

Learning how to learn will help a pilot flying any aircraft or simulator. Every time you fly, you should constantly be trying to figure out how to fly better. Your mind should be sensing how the aircraft is reacting. You should be practicing being aware. You should be analyzing whether there are any changes you could be making with your flying. You should be experimenting to discover whether a change to what you do, or how you do it, is more efficient. In other words, no matter what you are flying, you should constantly be learning how to be a better overall pilot.

No matter how talented you are, or how successful you already are, the more you improve, the better your chances of being successful in the future. No doubt you have known, or will know, pilots who thought they were so talented and knew so much about flying that they would be successful wherever they flew yet, eventually, reached a point where talent alone (i.e., without application and effort) was not enough to ensure ongoing success. If instead they had focused on learning and improving, they would have built on their advantage and continued to be successful.

An aircraft designer would never be successful at developing an aircraft without some plan. The same thing applies to learning and developing your flying. Without a plan, one of two things will happen: either no change and improvement will take place, or the wrong changes will take place. It's critical to establish objectives before every flight to ensure the correct changes take place. One reason military flying instructors ask their students to brief them on what they intend to practice before letting the student depart on solo flights is to ensure they have established objectives.

The point is, without making a change it is doubtful your flying will improve. It would, therefore, be a complete waste of time to head into the air without two or three specific objectives.

One of the best ways of establishing objectives for a flight is to figure out what questions you plan to ask yourself after the session. If, for example, you're going to ask where your aim point appears in the windscreen on final, what the rate of back stick application is when you begin your flare, and where the aircraft touches down on the runway, you have

> **PERFORMANCE TIP**
> *The more you learn, the better you get; the better you get, the more successful you will be. Focus on learning and success will follow.*

helped establish three specific objectives for the session. You have helped focus yourself. We will discuss this concept more in the next chapter on Self-Coaching.

Learning Stages

Whether it is learning to walk, throw a ball, or fly an aircraft, all human beings go through four stages when learning something new:

- Unconscious Incompetence
- Conscious Incompetence
- Conscious Competence
- Unconscious Competence

It may be easiest to relate these four stages to a baby learning to walk. In the beginning, a baby is at the *Unconscious Incompetence* stage; they haven't yet discovered that people can walk. In other words, they don't know what they don't know how to do.

At the *Conscious Incompetence* stage, the baby has now seen their parents walking and wants to, too, but can't. The baby knows what they don't know how to do.

The next stage, *Conscious Competence*, is where the child who is first learning to walk has to think about each and every step. They know what they know how to do, but are having to do it at the conscious level.

Finally, at the *Unconscious Competence* stage, the toddler no longer has to think about walking. It now happens automatically; they just do it. They don't think about what they know; they know and do, and don't have to think about it.

Every pilot goes through each of these same four stages with every new technique they learn. For example, consider every pilot's journey in learning how to land. In the beginning, we didn't even know the flare technique existed. We knew nothing about it and knew nothing about why we would do it. We were at the *Unconscious Incompetence* stage. When we became aware of the technique but didn't know how to do it, we were at the *Conscious Incompetence* stage. As we begin to practice flaring, we had to think through each detail of it: *Conscious Competence*. Finally, after practicing it over and over, it became automatic, a habit, and we no longer had to think about it, we just did it: *Unconscious Competence*. Obviously, to fly an aircraft competently and deal with added complications, such as varying wind conditions, we must reach this stage of flying at the subconscious level.

Most textbooks on learning strategies would highlight these same stages of learning. We would, however, like to add a fifth stage that the textbooks don't include. When it comes to flying aircraft, we would ask you to consider that there should be an *Unconscious Competence* with *Conscious Awareness* stage.

The *Unconscious Competence* stage is much like the experience of driving somewhere only to get there and not have been consciously aware of the stages of the journey. We're sure you have experienced that at least once in your life. You are driving completely on auto-pilot, and your mental programming is handling the chore while your conscious mind is off in another world. At this level, you are operating about as efficiently as possible, but you are *unaware*.

Now consider this scenario. You've been driving the same route to work for years. You drive to work, but sometimes don't even remember the process of doing it; you just arrive. You are certainly competent at driving to work, so much so that you don't even have to think about it consciously. At some stage, a highway construction crew builds a new road, a shortcut, which would cut your commute time in half. Because your conscious mind is off in another world, you don't notice. Your conscious mind is unaware.

Unless your conscious mind is aware, you will never make any improvements. Yes, you will continue to fly very well at the subconscious, programmed level but you will never upgrade the performance of that programming. Many times, this is the reason for a plateau on the learning curve; a complete unawareness of what could or should be improved.

The ultimate goal of any pilot is to fly at the subconscious level, relying on and trusting their programming, while using their conscious mind to observe and be aware of ways to improve their programming. It should be as if the conscious mind is looking over the pilot's shoulder, much like an in-cockpit camera would see it, watching for opportunities to upgrade the software.

The stages of learning explain how we learn.

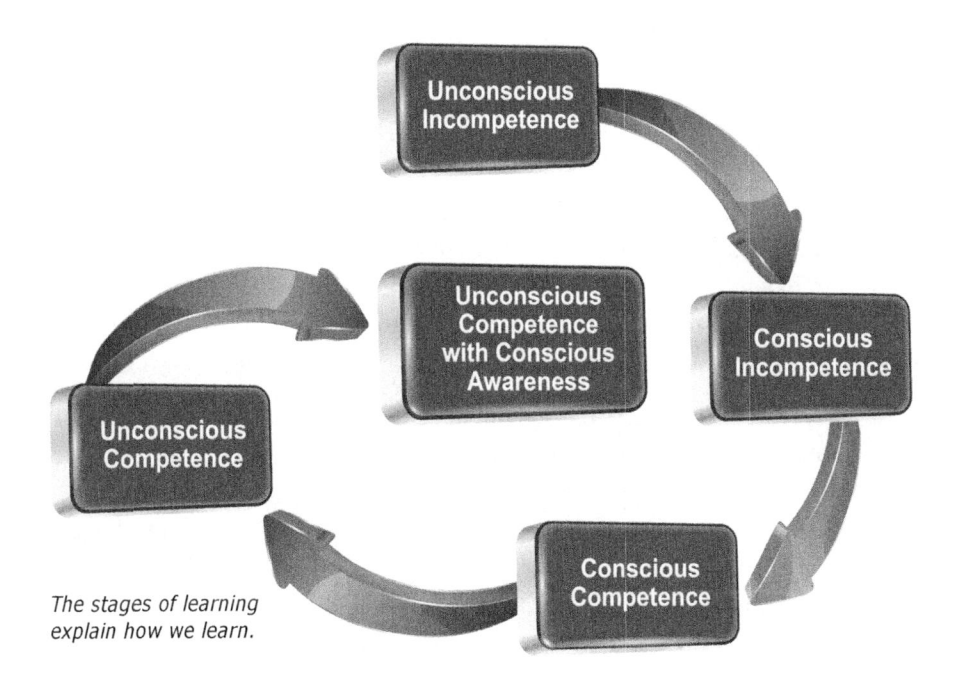

Learning From the Inside Out

Pilots and everyone else in the world learn in one of two ways: from the inside-out or from the outside-in.

Learning from the outside-in is what most people typically think of as learning. It is the method used within schools to teach us. Learning from the outside-in is what happens when you are "taught" something. You are told what to do or receive information; the information or knowledge comes from the outside (maybe from an instructor or coach) and "gets in" you. The "getting in" is not much of a problem, it is the staying in that is the challenge. Without it staying in, you haven't learned it at all.

On the other hand, learning from the inside out is when you discover or learn something for yourself, often through *guidance* or stimulation, rather than just being *told* what to do. This type of learning is so much faster, more efficient, and longer-lasting. In fact, once a pilot learns from the inside out, they will keep the knowledge forever. They will also be able to apply it in more complex scenarios and in conjunction with other techniques.

If you have ever wondered why some pilots seem to have a knack for knowing "instinctively" what to do in different scenarios, while others struggle with it, or need to be told by someone, this is the reason. Once a pilot truly understands *why* they need to fly the aircraft a certain way, they will have learned the feel for it and will be able to apply that to various scenarios they face. Without understanding why you're doing something, you won't have learned to do it at all.

Learning Through Osmosis

Tennis coaches in England have noticed for years a direct correlation between their students' abilities and the television coverage of Wimbledon. For a couple of weeks immediately following the tournament tennis players' performances improve significantly. Did they practice more, change their swing, or buy a new tennis racquet? No, they simply learned by watching.

All pilots learn through osmosis, the process of unconscious assimilation of skills or knowledge. The more exposure, the more they learn. You can learn a lot by watching other pilots. Of course, it makes sense that you should observe and learn from the best you possibly can. You will not learn as much from watching pilots who are not as good as you, although it is still possible to get something from that experience. In our research for this book, air force and airline instructors we have spoken to reported that their flying has improved markedly just by observing the common errors made by their students. By witnessing the same errors over and over again, they are more aware of where and why they occur and thus avoid making them themselves.

In these cases, they have learned by observation, appreciation, and imitation. Imitation is the ultimate learning technique. Copying, or modeling, is the most instinctive, simple, and natural way to learn. After all, that's exactly how we learned to do practically everything as a child and why flying instructors demonstrate new skills to their students.

If you want to learn a new skill, find someone who is very good at it. Getting advice from more experienced pilots or other knowledgeable individuals is a good practice. Many pilots will be flattered that you chose them to talk to and respect you for making the effort to improve. A word of warning, though: listen to the advice, but you be the judge. Just because it works for someone else doesn't mean it will for you or your aircraft.

Talk to and watch successful pilots. Even reading biographies of the best pilots in the world can help. Analyze what they are doing and saying. Obviously, you can't believe everything they say but listen. Many times they are not intentionally trying to lead you astray with wrong advice, but they may not know what it is that makes them successful. That's why it's important to watch for yourself and *think* deeply about all the aspects that come into play. Watch how other pilots complete a maneuver that may be a problem for you. They may have found the "secret" you haven't but be careful. They may be worse than you! When watching other pilots, notice what they do. Ask yourself why the aircraft or pilot are doing what they are doing? Understand the strategy and technique they are using.

When observing another pilot with the objective of learning, watch very carefully (follow through lightly on the controls if at all possible). As you watch, feel yourself moving in the same way and then practice by visually imitating. That doesn't mean just what the pilot is doing in the aircraft. How a pilot acts outside of the aircraft is just as important. "Acting as if..." you are one of your flying mentors outside the aircraft will improve your ability to fly like them.

Even if you aren't able to imitate someone perfectly, your attempts will increase your awareness of what skills, techniques and mental approach you still need to develop. Of course, you must first be prepared to imitate someone. You can't very well copy the advanced techniques of a World Champion before mastering the basics.

The Learning Formula

Perhaps the most important thing that you can take away from this entire chapter, if not the entire book, is what we call the Learning Formula. We cannot emphasize it enough: if you use it, this may just be the single most valuable piece of information in this entire book.

$$\textbf{MI} + \textbf{A} = \textbf{G}$$

Mental Imagery   **Awareness**   **Goal**

The Learning Formula.

In the Learning Formula, *"MI"* represents Mental Image, *"A"* represents Awareness, and *"G"* is your Goal (what you are trying to learn). If you use the Learning Formula each and every time you are trying to learn or improve upon something (which should be at least every time you head into the air, if not every moment of every day), you will be amazed at your ability to learn and improve.

In recent years, Phil had an extended period off work recovering from an injury sustained in a sporting accident. Due to the length of time he was away from work, he needed to do a check flight on his return. When he was initially checked out on the A330, his training emphasized the need to avoid long landings to protect against the possibility of runway overrun excursions. All his training had emphasized aiming to touchdown 1,000ft into the runway with a requirement to go-around if the aircraft was not down by 2,000ft. Subsequently, Phil had a firmly established mental image (program) for touching down as close to 1,000ft as possible.

During his check flight, Phil began his final approach with the aim to have the aircraft down by 1,000ft into the runway. In the flare, and in an attempt to impress the check pilot, Phil tried hard to finesse the aircraft onto the runway right at 1,000ft. After the extended absence, the finesse wasn't there, and he touched down just shy of 1,000ft. He thought he had done a reasonable job, as he had crossed the threshold at the correct height, touched down just shy of the point he was aiming for, and well before the 2,000ft limit emphasized in his initial training. He was totally surprised when the check pilot told him that he would need to go back to the simulator for retraining.

In his extended absence, the fleet had recorded numerous short landings. The check pilot explained that the emphasis now was that the touchdown must be between 1,000 and 2,000ft rather than at the beginning of the touchdown zone (Phil's paradigm). A subtle but important difference from Phil's initial training. The check pilot suggested using 1,500ft as a new aim point; right in the middle of the acceptable limits and giving a margin of error either way. This new aim point obviously made perfect sense but was a divergence from Phil's programming to that point. A change was required. So, what did Phil do to update his programming and how does this fit into the Learning Formula?

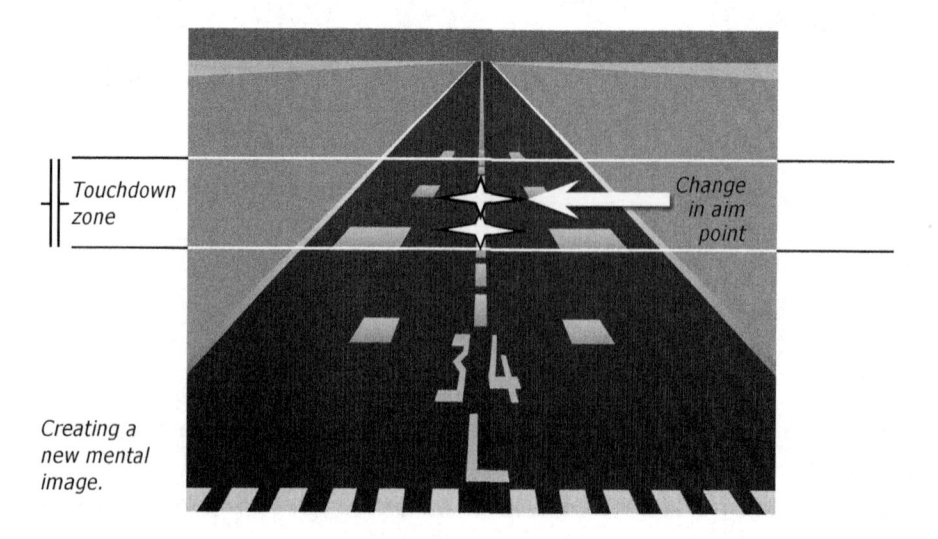

Creating a new mental image.

Fortunately, the check captain Phil had been flying with was able to provide him with all three components of the Learning Formula. Previously, Phil had been using an aim point slightly ahead of the far end of the 1,000ft markers on the runway to achieve main wheels touchdown at 1,000ft. To achieve the new Goal (the "G" in our Learning Formula) of main wheels touchdown at 1,500ft into the runway, the check pilot suggested Phil change his aim point to the beginning of the 1,500ft markers as a start point. This new aim point is the "MI," or Mental Image, element of our Learning Formula. This new mental image also gave Phil a start point for his mental imagery sessions before his retraining in the simulator. It gave him a clear mental image of what he would be looking for from the cockpit.

The final part of our Learning Formula is the "A" for Awareness. While mental imagery greatly increases our ability to learn and the speed at which learning takes place, being aware of the results gives us feedback on the effectiveness of our mental re-programming. Awareness speeds the process of creating or altering neural pathways. In our example, the check pilot provided Phil with the awareness cues required. He told Phil that every time he landed in his retraining, he needed to be aware of where he was touching down. Every time the aircraft touched down, he needed to note how deep into the runway it was and compare this to the desired goal of a 1,500ft touchdown. With this awareness, Phil would be able to adjust his mental image to achieve his goal of consistently touching down at 1,500ft. If his touchdowns were before 1,500ft, then the aim point needed to be deeper. Awareness of the main gear, touchdown point would help Phil adjust his mental image of his aim point until he found one that consistently worked. If he began to touchdown farther than 1,500ft, he'd need to bring the aim point closer to the threshold. The check pilot explained that while he could give Phil a start point for the aim point to use, the ultimate aim was for Phil to find an aim point that worked for him (modified with awareness) and to establish that as his new mental image.

Phil went away and conducted mental imagery sessions before his simulator retraining. He practiced using the new mental imagery, being aware of the actual touchdown point, and making adjustments to his mental image as required. Going into the simulator, this gave Phil both a new mental image as a start point and the programming to adjust the mental image as required if it wasn't exactly right.

The result? His first landing in the simulator was around the 1,400ft point - just shy of the goal but comfortably within the desired range. The check captain running the simulator session exclaimed, "Well, I can tell this is going to be a waste of time! There isn't any problem with your landings!" After a slight aim point (mental imagery) adjustment, the second landing was smack bang on 1,500ft. As the session was four hours long, the check captain explained that the original plan, to fix Phil's touchdown point, was now obsolete. They decided to up the ante. With the remaining hours, they practiced landings at the maximum crosswind and tailwind limits, low visibility, at heavy and light weights, and with various failure scenarios. Phil consistently touched down around the 1,500ft point and was subsequently returned to the line with an excellent write up for the session.

Whenever you establish a goal ("G") to make a change to your flying technique, use mental imagery to develop a clear "MI," and then head into the air and simply be aware. Build your awareness ("A") by asking yourself questions. Some awareness-building questions are: How was my aim point retention on final approach? Where did I touchdown? How close was I to the centerline? How much did my altitude vary in my steep turns? What was my speed tolerance on V2 on the climb out? How much g-force did I apply entering the maneuver? And so on. When used with the appropriate "MI," these "A"-building questions help you achieve your goals quickly, efficiently, safely, and enjoyably. We don't know of a faster way of learning anything than with utilization of the Learning Formula. Practice using it both in the air and on the ground.

> **PERFORMANCE TIP**
>
> $MI + A = G$

Let's use another example to demonstrate how it works. Let's say you're consistently getting slow in a particular part of a maneuver and you think it is because you either aren't exerting enough g-force while entering the maneuver or your speed is slow on entry. You could just tell yourself over and over again to "pull more g" or "enter faster." Will that work? Not likely. You could do some mental imagery, mental programming, of pulling a little harder or maybe flying a little faster. Will that work? Most likely, but it will take a while.

The reason it could take some time to take effect is that you may *only* have the "Mental Image" of what you *want* to do without awareness of what you *are* doing. Having determined the g-load and entry speed you think you need, you need to get back into the air and as you enter the maneuver ask yourself what the actual maximum g-load achieved was? How quickly did you apply the g-force? What was your *actual* entry speed? How close to the "Mental Image" of your "Goal" were you? Did this fix the speed problem mid-maneuver? If so, great! By combining the "Mental Image" with "Awareness," you have achieved your "Goal." If not then make changes. Try a slightly faster entry - what will this look, feel and sound like ("MI")? Alternatively, change the amount of g-force applied or its rate of application. Once again, what will this look, feel and sound like ("MI")? Try the maneuver again. What were your entry parameters this time ("A")? Using the Learning Formula, you can nibble away at achieving your desired performance/goal ("G") in a systematic and effective manner.

An example more relevant to a student pilot would be the goal ("G") of establishing a consistent flare height. Your instructor would be well able to provide you with the actual flare height required and the visual cues you would expect to see from the correct seating position inside the cockpit. The facts provided by your instructor provide you with the information needed to create the images required before beginning mental imagery sessions ("MI"). With the beginning of performing actual landings comes the awareness ("A"). After each landing, you would assess the actual flare height compared to the ideal flare height. When you are just starting out, your instructor could help with this part.

If a pilot has a clear "Mental Image" and an "Awareness" of what they are doing right now their mind will bring the two together. You may be surprised at how rare it is for a pilot to have both of these components. Some may have a clear "Mental Image" of what they want to accomplish, but have no "Awareness" of what they are currently doing. Others do not have a "Mental Image" of what they mostly want because they are overly aware of what they are currently doing. They are so focused on what they are doing wrong, they can't get the "Mental Image" of what they want.

Learning Curve

Every pilot, no matter how much natural talent they think they have or don't have, will continue to improve throughout their career. Even pilots reaching the ends of their professional flying careers are still improving in some areas. Unfortunately, other factors such as lack of motivation, desire, or a deterioration of physiological functions outweigh these improvements. How quickly and consistently you'll improve all depends on you and your operating environment.

One thing is clear, though. No two pilots have ever, or ever will, progress at the same rate. Every pilot's learning curve is different. Some pilots' learning curves are mostly steady upward inclines while others' are full of steps of all shapes and sizes. Some learn and progress quickly, others more slowly. It isn't an indication of how much talent a pilot has.

Every pilot's learning curve is different.

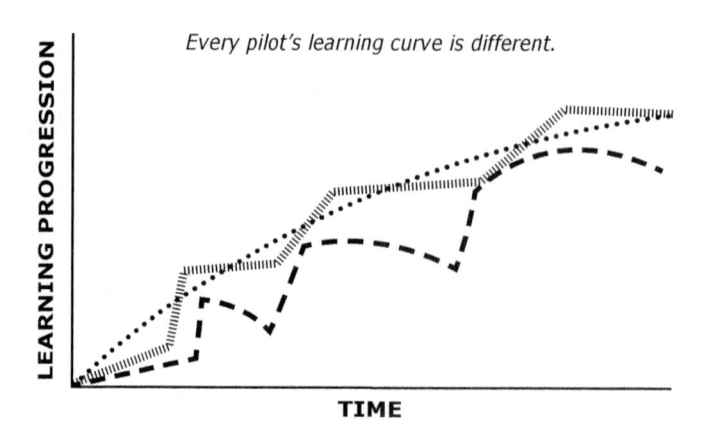

Very common among pilots are periods where the rate of progress and improvement seems to plateau with little to no improvement at all. Often, you and the people working with you become frustrated with the lack of progress and the plateau lasts longer. Most times, plateaus are followed by a sharp incline in progress if you can control the frustration and instead focus on improving your awareness.

Many times, the plateaus even appear to be steps backward. It's like one step back, two or three forward, one step back, two or three forward and so on. It's like the calm before the storm. In this case, the calm is the apparent lack of progress, and the storm is the whirlwind of learning.

If you think back to the learning stages, you'll understand why. Most often, for you to progress you must go back to the Conscious Competence stage where you're thinking through each step in a mechanical manner and this results in too much conscious thought and an apparent step backward. If you don't become frustrated by this, and with a little patience, this new technique, skill, or mental approach becomes part of your programming. You then progress to the Unconscious Competence stage where it becomes something that you seem to do naturally. At this point, there is a significant step up in the learning process

Watching children learn just about anything is an educational experience in itself. One thing we've learned from close observation of our children are the steps a child takes in the learning process. Just when there seems to be no progress whatsoever, bam! They master it. It certainly is not a steady progression. No, the learning curve is more like learning steps.

Ross relates a story about his daughter as an example. When she was four years old, Ross decided that it was the right time for her to learn to ride her bicycle without training wheels. Notice we said, "Ross decided." Ross went ahead and took off the training wheels and then spent the next few hours trying to get his daughter to learn how to keep her balance. It was certainly good exercise for Ross! The bottom line was, his daughter was neither willing nor ready to take this next step. The training wheels went back on.

A couple of months later she came to Ross and asked to have the training wheels taken off again. *She* had decided it was time to learn to ride a two-wheeler. Within minutes she had practically mastered it. Within thirty minutes she was showing Ross how she could ride up and down steep hills while holding on to the handlebars with one hand! There was no learning curve here, at least not when observed from the outside or probably even consciously on her part. It appeared as though her learning curve was completely flat then took a perfectly vertical step. In reality, even though neither she nor Ross was aware of what was going on, she was progressively learning. All of us closely follow the same pattern in our development.

The only pilots that do not seem to follow this pattern are the ones that get frustrated when they are on a plateau - the flat part of the curve. They get to that point where they don't feel they are getting any better, get upset or frustrated, and stay at that level or even get worse. The one piece of advice we can give about the learning process is that if it seems as if you're stuck at one level for some time, be patient. If you are using the strategies suggested here, you are about to make a big step up to the next level. You are almost ready to take the training wheels off.

One of Phil's flying instructor friends makes the following observation about plateaus. If he found a student was plateauing with a certain aspect of their flying training, they could lose motivation very fast. What he would do was move onto a new sequence and away from the particular task with which they were having trouble. This break served to re-engage his student with the improvement curve and restore their confidence in their ability to learn. He would then come back to the difficult sequence later or in another session entirely. For example, he had a student who just couldn't get his head around practice forced landings (PFLs), so he moved the emphasis of subsequent lessons to other sequences that the student grasped more readily and could focus on with enjoyment. The instructor would then "throw in" a PFL at the end of each lesson. Through exposure, the student eventually mastered PFLs but without the dread and stress that dedicated PFL lessons had been causing. You can equally apply this strategy of taking a break to your personal learning objectives.

PERFORMANCE TIP
If it seems you're not improving, you're about to.

Trial And Error

Is there anything wrong with making an error? Obviously, it depends on how much the error costs and who's paying for it, but if you want to improve or even just to perform at your very best right now, you must be willing to make a few errors. Why? Errors are valuable learning experiences when examined and used in the right manner.

As a very simple example of how recognizing errors can help us make improvements, consider a series of traffic patterns. If, on a particular day, your turn downwind is having you consistently rolling out on a wrong spacing then you either need to change the point you are beginning the turn or adjust the bank angle used for the given wind conditions. Likewise, for your turn onto final, if you are rolling out high or low on final then you would need to reconsider the power setting you are using to adjust the rate of descent around the base leg. If you constantly have to add or reduce power on final to acquire the correct glideslope, you need to reconsider your base turn point.

Every pilot makes errors. Being able to recognize and then analyze your errors is important. Until you can do that, you cannot even begin to correct them and improve. We're not suggesting that you dwell on them; just learn from them as you move ahead.

If you think about it, when we were young, trial and error was our most common and effective learning technique. For example, take the act of learning to walk. Imagine if, after falling the first few times you tried to walk, your parents said, "We don't want you trying that anymore; you always seem to fall." Or you, yourself, thinking, "I can't seem to get this right, so I won't bother trying anymore."

It's pretty absurd, right? However, in our lives we do this all the time. The second we make a mistake we tell ourselves (sometimes with subtlety, sometimes not so much) to never make that error again. How often does that help? Not very often! The point is that the more you resist errors, the more likely it is you'll make more.

One of the biggest differences between great pilots and not-so-great pilots is *not* that the former makes fewer errors. In fact, they both make about the same amount of mistakes. The difference is that the great pilots recover from, learn from, and know how to minimize the consequences of most errors. That only occurs when there is an atmosphere that allows errors and learning from them. Errors are simply a form of feedback that helps you home in on the desired goal. They are signals that help you continue to improve.

You must be able to observe what you are doing so you can improve on it. Errors should be examined to see what influenced or caused them. We're not suggesting you should dwell on every single mistake you ever make, but you should study the decisions or actions that led to the error being made to ensure it doesn't happen again.

Observing what you do is the key to learning from your errors. In fact, sometimes, let small errors happen; learn what corrections work, or don't. In some cases, by the time you notice an error, it may be too late to correct it. About all you can do then is minimize its effect. In fact, that is the key - minimizing the effect of errors and doing so as soon as possible.

When making a change to the way you fly, don't assume that if something doesn't work the first time that it will never work. It's a very common "error." Let's look at an example. You suspect that a technique change will make a significant improvement to your flying. You head into the air and, after a couple of attempts at the new technique, you don't see any improvement at all. Your conclusion is that the change to your technique won't work and you go back to your original method.

In many cases, the problem is not the change in technique but rather a lack of finesse with the new technique. It may be a case of blaming the wrong "cause." So, just because you can't make a small change in your technique work, don't discount it entirely. Rethink how you approach that maneuver. Maybe, by altering your technique slightly, using just a little more finesse, you can make the change in technique work, and it will have improved your flying as you initially suspected.

This being said, if a change does not work, you must also consider the possibility that you may have been working on an incorrect technique. If you suspect this at all, STOP! As we have already established, practicing the wrong technique will only reinforce the error, and you will find it very hard to unlearn the newly-entrenched bad habit. We suggest that if you try a technique that doesn't work after several attempts, it's time to change what you are doing or get some quality instruction. A good instructor should be able to identify and correct the error quickly.

You see, it is not a matter of making fewer errors, it is simply managing them. Once you realize this, you will undoubtedly make fewer of them. Why? In most cases,

PERFORMANCE TIP
If a change doesn't work the first time, rethink and retry.

you will stop trying to avoid making them. *Trying* not to make an error is a sure-fire way to ensure you make them. When you buy into the idea that your job is simply to minimize the effects of errors, life gets much easier.

Managing errors is a large part of competition aerobatics. It would be great to fly perfect aerobatic routines and never make mistakes, but that is fantasy. A competition aerobatics pilot Phil knows made the following observations: "Sometimes managing a mistake better than the next guy can win you the contest. Therefore, during practice, take your errors and turn them into learning exercises. If you make a mistake, think about and visualize how you would minimize the consequences, so that if it happens in competition, you already have a plan to execute. For example, if you make a major error coming out of a figure off axis, it might be best to exit the box, wear the penalty, and be set up perfectly for the next figure. For minor errors, like being too slow for the next figure, have a plan or idea as to how to manage that. Maybe let the next figure be compromised to ensure you are back on energy for the subsequent part of the sequence."

Mistakes are a natural process - don't fight them. Instead, consider what you can learn from an error, then re-program or see yourself doing it the correct way and forge ahead.

Unknown Maneuvers

"How do I fly a maneuver or sequence I have never flown before?" That's a question for which every student pilot would love the "secret" answer. So let's take a look at what you're up against when faced with a maneuver you've never flown before and see what you can do to discover that "secret." Approaching an "unknown maneuver," there are three interrelated factors that come into play:

1. your sensory awareness,

2. your existing database of information, and

3. aircraft control.

Sensory awareness and your database are somewhat interrelated. Your database of information comes from the hundreds, thousands, or millions of maneuvers you've flown in your life. Your database is primarily made up of visual images of what maneuvers look like, along with the resulting sensory information. If you lack sensory input, the database will not be as accurate or as useful as it could be. Of course, you could say your database is just experience (stick time) and you would be right to some extent. But why, then, do some pilots with little experience seem to have a larger database?

The better your sensory input, the better (richer) your database will be. In other words, your database is made up of tens, hundreds, thousands, or millions of reference points - ones you see, ones you feel, and ones you hear. It's as if the file of information on each maneuver is much thicker or deeper the more sensory information you have taken in. Our aircraft control comes into play in our ability to "dance" with the aircraft; handling the controls in such a way as to keep the aircraft on our desired flight path while flying within the aircraft's limits.

So how does this all come together in flying a new maneuver for the first time? Imagine flying a traffic pattern for the first time. For the vast majority of aircraft types, a traffic pattern is comprised of a take-off, a climb, a climbing turn, leveling off, flying straight and level, a level turn, a descending turn, speed control to an aim point, the arrest of a rate of descent, and finally braking to a full stop. By the time you fly a traffic pattern for the first time, you will have learned how to fly each of the parts of a traffic pattern in previous lessons. You, therefore, have a database already built up of how to fly each component of the traffic pattern, what it feels like, how it looks, how it sounds, and what control inputs are required. The components can be used to give you an idea of how a traffic pattern should look (and be flown during mental imagery) even though you've never flown one before.

Once you've flown a traffic pattern once, it is added to your database. Once it's in your database, you can refine your mental imagery. Using the information in your database, along with awareness, you can update the database without necessarily flying. Ask yourself: How accurate was I? How was my altitude maintenance? How about my speed control? My aim point retention on final? Close your eyes, relax, and picture a mental image of the maneuver but do more than just visualize it. Include more than just visual information. Also imagine how it feels and sounds. That is true mental imagery, mental programming.

The next time out, simply compare your Mental Image with your Awareness of how close you are to that Mental Image of the ideal maneuver; MI + A = G - the simplest, quickest and most effective way of learning and improving. The stronger, more vivid, your Mental Image, and the more Awareness you have, the more effective this will be and the easier it is to achieve your Goal.

Let's look at the real world example of one of the pilots we interviewed just after he had changed types from the Boeing 767 to the Airbus A320. How did he make the transition from landing a 767 to landing an A320? How did he move from the "known to the unknown"? Landing the A320 for the first time, he first sat down and thought about everything he could take from the things he knew from his 767 flying. His first landing in the A320 would be in a simulation of Sydney (Kingsford Smith). He knew what runway 16R in Sydney should look like and that it slopes down from the threshold. With reference to the FCOM, he knew the ballpark power settings and attitudes he would need to use. He also knew from the FCOM that he should reduce thrust to idle around 30ft and flare around 20ft. He presumed that his biggest challenges would be the avoiding the potential to lose his aim point retention below 500ft, using big pitch changes to correct, and over-controlling close to the ground which would increase his workload. He put all these known facts together and completed mental imagery sessions, utilizing what he did know and applying it to the unknown. It was a full mental rehearsal of what he needed to do, in the correct order, and with emphasis on making small, realistic corrections below 500ft. All he had to do, once he turned up to the simulator, was learn the nuances of flying the A320 and update his mental model, his database.

That's the "secret" to flying a maneuver you've never seen before. Start with your database and then use your awareness as you do it, so that you can add that to your mental image. Of course, that adds to your database and the whole cycle continues, getting better and better each and every time you fly. That is, really, the secret - improving every time out.

> **PERFORMANCE TIP**
> *Sensory input and awareness are the keys to flying proficiently, no matter what the maneuver is.*

If you look at every flight, every flight phase, and every maneuver from the perspective that you are soaking up information to add to your database, you will make immediate improvements in your flying. There are two reasons for this. First, when you give your brain more information to work with, it will produce a better result. Second, with this approach, it is more likely that you will relax and fly more at the subconscious level rather than "trying."

Learning Programs

If at all possible during either a simulator exercise, flight, or mental imagery session, try to end on a positive note. People tend to recall most vividly the last piece of information they encountered. This tendency to most deeply program into the brain what was most recently learned is called the "recency effect." In other words, you will recall and mentally replay your last session in the air more than any other. Mentally recalling and replaying creates programming. We're sure you would rather program a technically-correct, positive experience than the opposite.

The recency effect suggests how important it is that you recognize when you start to become tired, either physically or mentally, so that you can stop before you begin programming errors. The importance of stopping a session before we start to programming errors holds true for mental imagery sessions, simulator sessions, and flights. Remember, practice does not make perfect; only perfect practice makes perfect. It is far better to quit a session early than to practice and get good at making errors. Of course, if you physically or mentally tire before the end of a flight, you need to consider creating a fitness training program that will ensure it doesn't happen again.

Perhaps the greatest ice hockey player of all time, Wayne Gretzky, said, "No matter who you are, no matter how good an athlete you are, we're creatures of habit. The better your habits, the better they'll be in pressure situations." One of the roles of practice is to build better habits, better programming.

> **PERFORMANCE TIP**
> *The better your programming, the better you'll perform in pressure situations.*

Of course, just practicing flying around the sky may not be the most efficient use of time. As only perfect practice makes perfect, any amount of flight time you get should be focused. If not, you may just get better at doing the wrong thing, no matter what your level of flying.

Notice how the greatest athletes in any sport are commonly credited with having superior natural talent and yet they all seem to practice more, harder, and with greater focus than their competitors. It makes you wonder if all that natural talent is, in actuality, just more (and better) practice.

Basketball great Michael Jordan would show up for a game before other members of his team to practice his shots. When Tiger Woods was not winning everything in sight in 2001, he claimed it was because he was working on shots he would need specifically for the Masters later that year. Some people doubted his claim until he won the Masters again. Martina Navratilova, winner of 167 singles titles in tennis including a record nine Wimbledon titles, said, "Every great shot you hit, you've hit a bunch of times in practice."

The stories of Formula One driver Michael Schumacher's commitment to practice and being the best is part of his legend. After a day of testing

> **PERFORMANCE TIP**
> *Natural talent is just more (and better) practice.*

at Ferrari's test track, where he had just completed the equivalent of two full Grands Prix race lengths, he would spend a couple of hours in the gym, working out.

Philosopher Will Durant wrote, "We are what we repeatedly do, therefore excellence is not an act, but a habit." Numerous studies have shown that to achieve mastery in any complex field, a minimum of 10,000 hours of deliberate practice is the general requirement.

A study at Berlin's elite Academy of Music divided the school's violinists into three categories based on their potential. They then calculated the aggregate average time each group had spent practicing since they had begun playing the violin. All the subjects had started playing the violin at roughly the same age (five years old), but the amount of time they had spent practicing before arriving at the Academy varied greatly. By the time they had turned twenty years old, all the students with the potential to be virtuosos had totaled over 10,000 hours of practice and were averaging 30 hours of practice per week. Those students categorized as good enough to perform professionally, but not as virtuosos, had each totaled above 8,000 hours of practice. The students destined for amateur status, or to be music teachers, had totaled just over 4,000 hours each.

Other studies have added a very important point regarding the number of hours it takes someone to master an activity. It's not just how much practice you put in, but also what you practice that matters. The virtuosos not only practiced more, but they also practiced more difficult pieces. Looking at superstars in all activities, they practice the challenging things. For example, while many professional golfers practice by playing rounds, Tiger Woods is famous for having spent hours dropping a ball in a sand trap, stepping on it to make it even more difficult to hit, and then practicing hitting out from there.

The point is that you cannot expect to be a peak performance pilot if you don't practice and the more you practice the most challenging maneuvers, the better you'll be. Note that we have not mentioned any need for intrinsic talent. Study after study has found that it is the hours of practice that amount to mastery and not any genetic advantage. Practice is all about building better programming. The more you build better programming, the more credit you will receive for being "naturally talented."

We often believe the more we practice a skill or technique, over and over again, the better we'll get. This belief is not entirely true. In fact, every time you practice a technique incorrectly, you're increasing your chances of doing it wrong again. It's easy to become very experienced at repeating the same mistakes. So, don't practice too much at first or you're likely to develop incorrect patterns or movements. Instead, begin with shorter sessions, maintaining intense concentration and motivation. Continue practicing only while your concentration and interest are strong. If you begin to repeat an error, if your concentration or attention starts to fade, or if you start to become casual, then stop. Clear your head, get your concentration and motivation back, and then go again.

> **PERFORMANCE TIP**
> *What you practice is just as important as how much you practice.*

If you find that you have trained yourself in a bad technique, you will need to un-train it. You will need to reprogram yourself. In other words, if you are getting something wrong over and over, then it might mean you need to go back to basics and build up the technique again from the start.

General-aviation flying instructors are often inexperienced themselves. As a result, many pilots are not taught well in the ab initio phases. They carry these problems through to advanced flying such as aerobatics or instrument flying. If you find that your training has been substandard, it might be worth revisiting some relevant basic skills. For example, you won't fly good formation if you never learned how to coordinate rudder and aileron correctly or how to trim.

A competition aerobatic pilot we spoke with relayed a story of how he was taught poor technique and procedures during his ab initio stall training. He didn't realize this until he got serious about aerobatics. He had revisited his understanding of stalling by downloading articles written by people who knew what they were talking about and reeducated himself about the basics.

Self-Coaching

If you wanted to be the absolute best pilot you possibly could be, ideally every time you went into the air, you would take a qualified instructor with you to continually improve your performance. However, this is quite clearly impractical due to financial constraints and the fact there aren't enough qualified instructors in existence to cover every pilot. Therefore, you need to learn to coach yourself.

Self-coaching is the technique of guiding yourself towards maximizing your performance and improvement in everything you do. Part of self-coaching is self-debriefing. The primary objective of debriefing is to increase your awareness. As we discussed in the previous chapter, without awareness, you will have a difficult time knowing what you should work on to improve or if you are making any progress.

No matter what level or type of flying you are involved in, after every flight, you should debrief. This debriefing may only take a minute or two, or it could last for hours. Your main aim in debriefing is to determine what the objectives should be for the next flight to make further improvements.

One of Phil's friends, an airline captain, debriefs with his first officer after every sector by asking, "What did we do well?" and "What could we do better?" To avoid the emphasis being on the approach and landing (the most recent event in the flight), he finds it valuable to give himself time to replay the entire flight mentally for a minute or two before debriefing. He then breaks the debriefing down by the phase of flight.

To fundamentally improve your performance as a pilot, you should keep a record or journal with the details of each and every flight. As you go through this process, you will build your awareness of what both you and the aircraft are doing. The act of writing it down leads to a fuller awareness level. Without that awareness, you will not have the information you require to fly better nor will you have an awareness of what you need to change to improve your flying.

One of the best ways to debrief is to ask yourself questions and rate your performance and abilities in a variety of areas after each session. We've listed some example questions in Appendix B; ones you could ask after each flight and ones to ask yourself before you even get to the airport. As you go through the process of digging deep in the attempt to answer them, you will coach yourself to a much higher level of performance behind the controls of an aircraft. The overall objective of these questions is to help you become more aware of exactly what you are doing. If you are aware of what you are doing now and know what you want to be doing differently or better, you will quickly and naturally make the necessary improvements.

To help facilitate debriefing, you could even make up a debrief form that includes all the areas on which you choose to assess your flying. Where applicable, you could even base your personal debrief form on the actual forms used by Designated Pilot Examiners/Examiners of Airmen/Departmental Examiners when they conduct practical flight tests for the issuance or renewal of licenses and rating. Obviously, you can debrief yourself without a form but physically writing notes will help you gain more from the strategy. The physical act of writing something seems to increase your

Keep a journal of your self-coaching debriefs.

awareness level as well as being more accurate. You will be more honest with yourself when you rate your flight on paper. You can also use these records to learn from as you look back at them when preparing for your next lesson, flight test, or simulator session or when you are having a problem with a specific area of your flying.

Another aid to debriefing is to use diagrams of the maneuvers flown and debrief with them. Make notes on the diagrams, writing down details on what the aircraft is doing: speeds, attitudes, power settings, g-forces, control forces, where you are looking, what you can hear, what you feel, etc.

Rate your flying on a scale of 1 to 10 in each maneuver with a "10" representing a perfectly-flown maneuver and "1" being well away from that. The exact number you put on "how close to perfection" you were for each maneuver is not important. Every pilot will perceive perfection as something a little different, so it is not something that you could compare from one pilot to another. The goal is simply to help you become fully aware of whether you are flying every maneuver to the best of your current ability. Through the exercise of putting a number on how close to perfection you are flying the aircraft in each maneuver, you will become completely aware of where there is room for improvement.

The interesting thing is that most pilots will have to recalibrate their ratings as they improve. Often, you will believe you are flying at a "9" or "10" on the scale for a little while. Then, with a bit more experience, and a better sense or feel, what you once perceived as a "10" will only be a "7."

Before each flight, write down the objectives you have established for each session and what flying techniques or plans you need to use to achieve them. After each flight, make comments on what the results of the flight were. One of your key objectives should be to ensure you never make the same mistake twice or have to learn the same thing twice. Extensive notes are therefore essential in this journey.

When you are writing your notes, make sure that you express any instructions or thoughts in a positively-framed manner. Instead of making a list of things you did wrong, frame your notes to reflect what you want to do next time. For example, "Don't balloon in the landing flare" could be rephrased as, "When flaring, look to the end of the runway for more visual cues for arresting the rate of descent for touchdown." "Don't forget to disarm the spoilers when you select the flaps to zero" could be rephrased as, "Disarm spoilers with flaps zero selection." In a later part of the book, we will explain why a positive reference is so important.

You should make notes of all the things you have learned each flight. If that isn't a pretty extensive list, you are not doing your job. Regardless of how much experience you have, you will always be learning something new if you are aware. Obviously, writing down what you have learned will reduce the chances of you forgetting and having to learn the lesson all over again.

Serious competition aerobatic pilots use a ground-based coach who critiques their sequences into a voice or video recorder while observing the flight. Alternatively, if the student has the "head space," the coach sometimes uses a radio to commentate, giving tips or instruction in real time. Either of these methods would help an aerobatic pilot compile their post-session notes.

If at all possible, to avoid comparing yourself to others, go through the debrief process before learning how your performance rated in a flight test or competitive environment. This methodology will improve the accuracy of your awareness and feedback.

Finally, you should rate your overall performance on a scale of 1 to 10 for each flight and make a note of how you felt and what you did leading up to it. That way, over time, a pattern will begin to emerge; one that spells out a routine or ritual that will lead to consistently great performances. For example, if you notice that whenever you physically warm-up before flying, or that a certain phrase used by you or another crew member seems to lead to "9" performances, you know what you must continue to do in the future.

PERFORMANCE TIP
Increase your awareness by debriefing.

To emphasize the power of ritual to great athletes, one need look no further than the most successful Olympian of all time, Michael Phelps. Phelps, winner of a record 28 medals (23 gold), has an extensively-reported on race day ritual. His routine includes:

- what he eats for breakfast,
- watching movies to either psych-up or relax,
- meditative relaxation immediately before a race, and
- "putting in his videotape" - mental imagery of swimming perfectly and a variety of possible difficulties he may experience during a race.

At the pool, Phelps routine continues with a timed countdown including:

- stretching,

- a standard swimming warm up,
- changing into his race suit,
- donning his headset to listen to music to relax and get into his own world, and finally,
- a set routine on the blocks.

It becomes much easier to develop a pre-flight ritual that will lead to a great performance if you make a note of factors affecting your performance. For examples, your state of mind, energy level, intensity, what you have eaten over the past day or two, who has been around you and what they have said, and how confident or nervous you felt. Without writing it down, it's easy to miss patterns.

Preparation and Practice

Flying an aircraft is a series of compromises: atmospheric conditions change, fuel and passenger loads vary, and traffic and subsequent air traffic control restrictions are never the same two traffic patterns in a row let alone for two entire flights. There is also the human element: who we are flying with, their personalities, and their adherence (or otherwise) to standard operating procedures. There are hundreds, perhaps thousands, of compromises and decisions to be made every flight. You constantly have to monitor and adjust your flying to best suit the conditions and variables as they present themselves to you. Practically every moment of the flight you have to consider and reconsider what your strategy should be.

The pilot that chooses the best compromises most often performs at the highest level in comparison to their peers. A pilot whose mind is best prepared is more likely to make the ultimate compromises.

Preparation

Our experience tells us that the most successful pilots, no matter what the level, are the ones who prepare more and better than the others. We doubt you'll often find a great pilot who doesn't like things to be organized, controlled, disciplined, and prepared. Flying is all about control and discipline.

Most, if not all, great pilots control their lives and everything around them. Their attention to detail is paramount. That includes their diet, physical exercise program, mental training program, ensuring their safety equipment is clean and so on.

Mental preparation for flying, as in sport, is a key element. People often talk about the "natural talent" of athletes like Michael Schumacher, Michael Jordan, Wayne Gretzky, and Tiger Woods. If there is one thing all these great athletes have in common it is how hard they worked, how much they practiced and the amount of time and effort they put into preparing for their sport.

There is a true story about Ayrton Senna, arguably one of the greatest race car drivers of all time, which is a great example of how true natural talent mostly comes from hard work. A couple of hours after winning his first Formula One Grand Prix in Portugal in 1985, Senna was seen driving around the track in a street car. He had totally dominated the entire race with one of his magical performances in the rain, so what was he doing driving the track in a road car? Trying to figure out how he could have performed even better. That's commitment to being the best. That's preparation. That is what is often confused for natural talent.

Winners go way out of their way to ensure they have prepared in every way possible. Michael Jordan would often show up early for a game, well before his teammates arrived, and practice his three-point shot. If someone of Jordan's abilities knew the value of practice and preparation, shouldn't you?

All the skills and techniques in the world are not going to make you perform if you aren't suitably mentally prepared. What you do to prepare mentally before a flight is somewhat individual. It's difficult for us to tell you what will work for you. You have to experiment to find out for yourself what works and what doesn't. For example, for some competition aerobatic pilots, sitting alone and not talking to anyone is the trick. For others, that results in more nervousness. Instead, talking with their friends or their crew takes their mind off the pressure of the next flight.

Flying hours are valuable. Make them count. If possible, we strongly suggest giving yourself a few minutes immediately before each flight to sit and think about what you've planned to change or achieve. Make a plan and then work to that plan.

Also, take the time to consider what you will do if things don't go according to the plan. For example, what happens if you fall out of the new maneuver you are about to practice? Having pre-considered your actions enables you to be mentally prepared for the consequences. It also helps your confidence level because you've prepared, you have it under control, and it doesn't take you by surprise.

Many pilots wonder how they can visualize every possible scenario that could happen. You can't. The same applies to using mental imagery for mentally preparing to fly an aircraft you have never flown before. How can you visualize something when you have no idea of how it would possibly look? In your preparation, you want to use a kind of open-ended mental imagery where you actualize yourself as being open and ready for anything. It's not that you imagine every possible scenario, but that you are ready and make the right moves no matter what happens.

> **PERFORMANCE TIP**
> *Preparation is not just one thing; it's everything.*

Practice

Your mental approach to practice and testing is important. There is no point in ever getting airborne if you're not going to fly at 100%. There is no reason ever to think that a sloppy sequence is "good enough." You don't want to make "good enough" a habit. The only way to ensure that doesn't happen is always to fly at 100%.

A lot of pilots practice bad habits when flying outside of the simulator or testing environment. They don't hold the controls properly or use the controls smoothly, and they are slack with their standard operating procedures, altimetry, radiotelephony, and standard calls. How do they expect to fly any differently during a test when they've just programmed those techniques into their heads? It's the same with sport. What do you think would happen if a tennis pro practiced hitting one-handed backhands all year and then went to Wimbledon and played using a two-handed backhand?

If you're practicing for a test, you want to simulate the testing environment as closely as possible as often as possible. To be successful in your flight tests you want the same intensity in your practice sessions as you do in the test; you should be 100% focused and have 100% concentration. If you practice at 99%, that's how you will perform in a test. It's very difficult to get back to 100%.

> **PERFORMANCE TIP**
> *Practice how you plan to test and then you'll test as you practiced.*

A pilot can practice many of the techniques required to ace their tests during their everyday flying. Practice always being smooth and consistent, and not just on the primary flight controls; this applies equally to braking, using the throttles or thrust levers, rolling into and out of turns and keeping the aircraft balanced.

You don't have to do this quickly either; this is not just physical practice. Just like a golfer or tennis player "grooves" their swing, you are "grooving" your aircraft control techniques. Each time you apply the brakes or move the controls your actions are being "programmed" into your brain. The more your technique is "programmed," the easier, smoother and more natural it will be in the heat of the battle of a test or license renewal.

Treat practice and tests with the same respect and intensity. When you practice, it should be with the same mental focus and determination as if it were in a test. This focus programs your mind so that, under actual test conditions, you instinctively respond. During a test, you will be as relaxed and calm as if you were practicing.

Performance State of Mind

Your state of mind covers many areas: your levels of anxiety, happiness, anger, nervousness, fear, passion, enthusiasm, empathy, and so on. Your state of mind plays a huge role in your level of performance. In fact, it's critical, right?

So, where does our state of mind typically originate? It originates from "out there;" things that happen to us, things that people say to us and external happenings (positive or negative).

What do we typically focus on when we're in a poor state of mind? The rotten state of mind we're in. We say things like: "I'm just in a bad mood today" or "I got up on the wrong side of the bed this morning." Of course, that just leads to a further decline of our state of mind. In other words, it spirals out of control.

If you want to be successful, you must control your emotional or mental state of mind. If you are excited, nervous, depressed, stressed, distracted or angry, you may not be mentally effective. Your decision-making will slow and your mind will not be focused.

Replaying Past Successes

Unfortunately, for most pilots their state of mind is something that just happens and they have little to no control over it. It is rare for a pilot to have a defined process or ritual for triggering the ideal performance state of mind. In other words, they either get into a great state of mind, or they don't; either way, it is almost totally by accident.

You can hope that you show up for each flight in the right state of mind (but hoping is not a very effective strategy), or you can learn to trigger a performance state of mind. So, how do you induce a performance state of mind?

The best technique we know of is to simply ask yourself to recall, and replay in your mind, a great past performance. There is nothing that will build or improve your confidence as much as a little success. Fortunately, these successes do not necessarily have to be piloting an aircraft. You should feed off your successes no matter where and when they are in your life.

Whether it's success playing another sport, a positive business experience, participation in a hobby or a great personal relationship experience, recalling past successes in anything will trigger a positive state of mind. So, focus on past successes. See them vividly in your mind's eye. Replay every detail about those performances from a technique point of view, how you felt, your emotions, and your state of mind before, during, and afterward. Anything that results in being extremely positive, happy, energized, and calm will do the trick.

In his role as a performance coach, Ross has used this technique often when coaching race car drivers, particularly just before a qualifying session. He likes to find out beforehand about a great performance in the driver's past and then ask them to replay the story just before qualifying. He's had drivers relate stories about a past hockey or soccer game, a previous qualifying session or race, or a positive business

Vividly recall past successes to trigger a performance state of mind.

experience. In each case, he could see on their faces that they were in a positive, performance state of mind after telling their story.

At one stage of his career as a professional race car driver, Ross was averaging a gain of six places during the first two laps of a race. At one round of the World Sports Car Championship Ross had qualified in tenth position but at the end of the first lap was in second position. Before subsequent races in the series, he kept replaying that start over and over in his mind, and he kept getting great starts. He knew before the start of every race that he was going to pass at least four or five cars on the first lap. Replaying those successes in his head led to many more because Ross was in a performance state of mind.

> **PERFORMANCE TIP**
> *Replay past successes to trigger a performance state of mind.*

Focus

Is there any danger in thinking about the past? There certainly can be. Anytime you spend focusing your attention on what has happened in the past is time that your attention is not being spent focusing on what is happening right now in the present.

Can you do anything about what has happened in the past? You can't, absolutely not. If you make a mistake on the runway during take-off, does thinking about that while leveling off at acceleration altitude help or hinder? Hinder for sure. Does getting upset about the lack of support coming from the support pilot's seat help? No. The second you make an error or something less than favorable happens, forget it. What you did, or what another pilot did, is not important now.

Can you do anything about what is going to happen in the future? Yes. How? You do this by the actions you are taking right now. When you focus your attention on the present, you increase your chances of performing at the level that will result in the goals you have set.

"*Do not think about a pink elephant!*"

Thoughts

As you read this sentence, do not think about a pink elephant. Do not think about a pink elephant! So, what are you thinking about right now? You're thinking about a pink elephant, right? In fact, it is impossible not to think about something. The only way you cannot think or focus on something you *don't* want is to think or focus on something you *do* want.

For example, as you sit on the flight deck if you are having thoughts like "don't mess up the landing this time," or "don't over-control," you are setting yourself up to do the complete opposite. In these examples, you have made your brain focused on messing up the landing and over-controlling! Pilot-induced oscillations here we come!

Obviously, negative thoughts like this could also be implanted in your consciousness by others: your flying instructor, your support pilot, your ground crew, etc. It would be ideal if everyone around you could be aware that what they say can affect your performance but that is not always practical. So you must have a plan or strategy to manage whatever anyone says or does.

In the case of not *not* thinking about something someone says, the strategy is fairly simple. To demonstrate, imagine a blue elephant. Whenever anyone says "pink elephant" imagine a blue elephant. What you have done is developed a Pre-Planned Thought (PPT). Now when we say, "don't think about a pink elephant," what do you see in your head? Hopefully, you thought of a blue elephant! If you didn't, you need to practice this some more.

You must have a PPT ready and available to take on any unwanted thoughts thrown at you, either intentionally or not. You need to develop a PPT and practice using it. Perhaps your PPT could be something similar to "smooth and confident." Whenever anyone says anything that could distract your focus, or get you focusing on something you don't want, simply say "smooth and confident" to yourself. When you say this phrase, you immediately conjure up an image of flying an aircraft smoothly and confidently. Isn't this exactly what a peak performance pilot would do? Through practice, the image will become very strong and vivid, and one that will take the place of practically anything anyone says or does. You don't have to use our example of "smooth and confident." You can use anything you like that projects the thought patterns and behaviors you would like to emulate.

PERFORMANCE TIP
Develop and use a Pre-Planned Thought (PPT).

Behind the controls of your aircraft, have you ever thought to yourself, "That was a stupid mistake" or, "Why did I over-control the rudder on that V1 cut?" Did any of those thoughts do you any good? We doubt it. In fact, we bet they did more harm than good.

A study showed that the average person has approximately 66,000 thoughts every day with 70 to 80% of those being negative. We doubt that this study included any champion athletes! We would suggest that at least 70 to 80% of their thoughts are positive.

Focusing on negative thoughts or ideas will most likely adversely affect your performance. Thoughts like, "if I don't apply g-force quickly enough I'm going to run out of energy" takes some concentration and attention away from the ideal, positive thought like "I need to apply five-g as quickly as possible as I enter the maneuver."

If you are going to have some thoughts while flying (and there is no doubt you will - at least your passengers hope so!) make them non-judgmental thoughts. Turn everything you can into a positive. If you take every situation that other pilots consider a problem or unpleasant (bad weather, crosswinds, complex sequences, too much traffic, etc.) and turn them into positive challenges, you will perform better. Turn them into "watch this" situations, a chance to tackle a challenge head on and demonstrate your capabilities. For example, just by saying you love instrument flying over and over again will make you a better instrument pilot. It's simply a matter of turning negative thoughts and questions into positive talk.

> **PERFORMANCE TIP**
> *Make your thoughts non-judgmental.*

In the chapter on Self-Coaching, we have already suggested that negatively-phrased instructions and thoughts should be replaced with positively-framed ones when writing self-briefing notes.

You can apply this same theory to where you look when you are flying. For example, if you have identified an issue with not looking far enough ahead when landing, or not taking in a wide visual picture from your peripheral vision, just thinking to yourself not to fixate on the threshold or aim point will not do any good.

The amazing thing about the mind is that if you put an image or thought into it, your mind will find some way to make it happen. When you say to yourself, "Don't fixate on the aim point," your mind only really registers the "fixate on the aim point" part of the message. Your mind fixates on the aim point even to the exclusion of lifting your eyes to the end of the runway for the flare or taking into account all the sensory information available in your peripheral vision.

So, instead of thinking, "Don't fixate on the aim point," you should think, "Look towards the end of the runway." The only way of not thinking or

> **PERFORMANCE TIP**
> *Replace negatively-phrased instructions and thoughts with positively-framed ones. Focus on what you want.*

looking at what you don't want to think or look at is to think or look at what you do want; this might sound like a mouthful, but it is completely true. Go back and read it again.

Good skiers use this same strategy for avoiding rocks in the snow. Instead of focusing on the rocks (where they don't want to go), they focus on where they do want to go (a path between the rocks). By focusing on a path between the rocks, their mind subconsciously orders signals to their legs to steer the skis to follow the path to avoid the rocks.

Consistency and Concentration

The mark of a great pilot is consistency. When you first start flying, you must concentrate on being consistent. Your goal should be to operate to the best of your ability consistently, to perform at your peak. Work on always being smooth and consistent with your technique, session after session.

To do that, you must remember what you did and keep doing it session after session or flight after flight. That is not as easy as it sounds, but it's not until you fly with consistency that you can begin to work on really honing your skills to their finest level.

If you want to change something about your flying technique, how are you going to know if it has improved your overall performance if you're not already flying at a consistently standard? For example, if you can't consistently bring the aircraft in over the threshold at 50 feet, how do you know if a change to your flare technique is what has made the difference to your touchdown point or the smoothness of your landings?

Concentration is the key to consistency. When you lose concentration, your flying suffers. Have you ever noticed that after a certain time airborne, a certain phase of flight, or maybe towards the end of a flying lesson or simulator session, mistakes tend to occur?

When you physically tire, your concentration level suffers. If you notice inaccuracies starting to creep in, or that you are making errors, it may be that you have become physically tired and have begun to lose concentration.

When you identify that you have started to lose concentration, you may find it helpful to talk yourself through what you are trying to do. Internally direct your flying as an instructor would. Even better, if you are in a multi-crew environment, explain out loud what you are doing. Not only does this share more information, and aid in a cockpit resource management sense, it helps you to regain concentration. Usually, after a few minutes of talking yourself around the sky, you're back to flying subconsciously.

The best pilots lose their concentration as much as any other, but what they do better is regain it much quicker. You can make use of your PPT to help trigger concentration or quickly regain it if it's lost.

There is a limit to how much a pilot can concentrate on, though. You can very easily concentrate too much on one particular area when you need to spread it over more than one. When trying to improve a particular facet of your flying, work on one concentration area at a time. Don't go out with the intention of perfecting all phases of your flying and eliminating all weak areas in a single session. Your brain cannot handle everything at once. Instead, decide on two or three areas at most. Choose two or three of the most important things that will help make you a better pilot and then work on them.

It takes more concentration to keep something from happening than it does to make something happen. Don't be concerned with making an error. You should be willing to make errors (that is *willing* to, not *wanting* to). As we discussed in the Learning chapter, the more you concentrate on resisting errors, the more likely it is you will make them. So relax!

Don't let a mistake take your concentration away. Everyone makes mistakes. Learn from them and then forget them. It's important when you make an error to quickly understand why it happened so you can ensure it doesn't happen again, and then concentrate on what's happening next.

Although we have emphasized always getting airborne with learning objectives, sometimes a constant focus on improvement may dull your joy of flying. If this is the case, just go and fly without thinking about improving or worrying about making mistakes. Relax and just "let it flow."

Intensity Level

Every time you get behind the controls of an aircraft, you must perform at the same intensity level you want when it is going to count the most, for example, in a flight test or competition. There is no point practicing in a casual, "I don't care how I do this flight; it's a solo, and no one is watching; this flight is not very important," attitude and then expect to perform any differently when it does count. Remember, practice is programming. If you program flying with a low-intensity level, that's how you'll perform in the heat of the battle.

PERFORMANCE TIP
Practice is programming.

You need to determine what level of "psyching" results in your best performance. Each pilot has an optimum level of being psyched - the optimum level of emotions, tension, anxiety, nervousness, and energy. The key is to be aware of what emotional state results in a superior or peak performance and then use that knowledge to program the corresponding emotional state so that you can recreate it over and over again.

Some pilots need to psych themselves up while others must calm themselves down. Not being energized or intense is not a problem for many people in a sport or profession like flying, but it is not uncommon for pilots to be too calm, relaxed, or even fatigued. If you find you are routinely too calm or relaxed before a flight, you need a program for energizing. Some things you could consider are:

- seeing yourself alive and energized,
- warm-up exercises (cross-crawls),
- clenching your fists,
- flexing your muscles,
- yelling or screaming,
- using powerful words,
- getting your heart pumping,
- taking rapid deep breaths, or
- listening to loud rock music.

One technique we recommend to trigger a calm mental intensity is this: every time you make the walk across the flight line or down the aerobridge to your aircraft, whether on a solo flight, a lesson, or on a test, act like you mean business. Give your all in every phase of flight from flight planning, to walk around, to engine start, to taxi - every aspect of every phase. Be intense (but not tense!). This intensity will ensure you mentally get up to speed straight away. It will dial up your intensity level. It sets a tone for you and sends a message to any observers that you're here to do business.

On the other hand, you don't need to be too psyched-up. You need to be calm, relaxed and focused. Being too psyched-up makes you overly excited and therefore less effective. You want to fly with a "clean mind," not one cluttered with useless thoughts.

Having no thoughts at all is far more desirable than having a mind full of them. A mind full of thoughts is one that will not react instantaneously and naturally. In the practice of Zen, they encourage an empty or beginner's mind. In his book, *Zen Mind, Beginner's Mind*, Suzuki Roshi writes, "If your mind is empty, it is always ready for anything; it is open to everything. In the beginner's mind there are many possibilities; in the expert's mind there are few."

Once you get behind the controls, it doesn't matter what is happening outside the aircraft. All that matters is you, the aircraft, and the task at hand. Forget everything else. Possibly, this is why many pilots find flying so relaxing. They can forget absolutely everything else that is happening in their lives.

Effort

Another thing people who perform physical skills to a high standard tend to have in common is a relaxed demeanor. Have you ever noticed how practically every great athletic performance looks almost easy or effortless? It is not a coincidence that most athletes have that appearance when performing at their best.

Great performances, and therefore the best results, are always achieved when you use the right amount of effort in the right places. This right amount of effort is usually less than you think necessary. Like what we said about psychomotor skills, the less *unnecessary* effort you spend, the more successful you will be. The key is to use *appropriate* effort - economy of movement.

Doing the wrong thing with more effort rarely results in a good performance. Great pilots use less effort to produce great performances and great results. The more intense the competition or test, the more they relax and just let it happen.

> **PERFORMANCE TIP**
> *Relax, use less effort, and just let it happen.*

Trying

Your goal in reading this book is most likely to improve your flying by being better at what you do behind the controls. Unfortunately, many pilots with this goal *try* to be better. The result is rarely what the pilot wants.

"Try" is a very negative word. Entertainers who use neuro-linguistic programming (NLP) or stage hypnosis consider "try" to be a failure word and will often use the word "try" in their patter when they want their subject to fail to do something. For example, if a hypnotist is hypnotizing a subject to believe that they cannot move they will use phrases like, "try and pull your hands apart, try and move." Trying implies the possibility of failure and the hypnotized subject finds that they cannot move. When instructed that they "can" start to feel their hands coming apart and their bodies start moving, they can move again.

Yoda, the Star Wars character, summed it up best when he said, "Do, or do not. There is no try." Either do something or don't do something. There is no point in trying to do something. By the very definition of the word, trying gives you a way out - an excuse. Trying means "to attempt." To us, that doesn't sound very positive; it doesn't to your brain either.

One of the most common causes of errors, particularly under pressure, is "trying." Rarely does anyone, let alone a pilot, perform at their best when "trying." Trying is a conscious act and not one that leads to maximum performance. Not only is trying not an automatic, programmed act but the second you try your body tenses. The second you become tense, you are unable to perform smoothly and your performance suffers.

Flying an aircraft well (performing at your personal 100%) comes from flying subconsciously. It comes from the "programming" in your brain. *Trying* to fly better is just like *trying* to make a computer do something without having installed any software. It's just not going to happen. Trying is flying consciously. Instead, focus on giving your bio-computer more input. Focus on what you can see, feel and hear. Become aware and visualize the act of flying.

You must learn to relax and let your body and the aircraft "flow." Fly naturally, subconsciously. Don't force it. Relax and just let it happen. Focus on your performance.

Flow

We think everyone has experienced being "in the flow" at some time in their life. It may have been while doing a job, playing a sport or musical instrument, or just going about a normal day. It's that time when everything just seems to go right, everything you do works perfectly, almost without thinking about it. Unfortunately, everyone has probably experienced the opposite when, no matter how hard you try, it just doesn't seem to work.

With experience ("seat time") comes flow. Flow is when you are flying subconsciously, naturally, without trying. Everything you do becomes automatic. You can't try to get in the flow. It comes naturally, subconsciously. Just let yourself feel like you're part of the aircraft, one with the aircraft. You know when you're in the flow; it feels great.

We bet that every time you've ever been in the flow or zone in the past, there were two factors at play: you felt challenged, and you had confidence in your ability to handle the challenge. In fact, a combination of challenge and belief in yourself will do more for triggering flow than just about anything else.

If you're not feeling challenged, you'll almost feel bored. You're unlikely to have the intensity it takes to get into the flow and perform at your peak. Of course, if the challenge seems too great, too daunting, it's also unlikely you'll perform at your best. You'll feel overwhelmed and likely not have the inner belief that you can handle the challenge. On the other hand, if you feel challenged by what you're doing, and you feel confident that you can overcome the challenge, you're more likely to perform in the flow.

Framing flying as a tough challenge, but one you can handle, will help you perform better. Sometimes it's a matter of doing just that: looking at it (framing it) as not easy but something you can handle, something not beyond your capabilities. With that mindset, you're more likely to get into the flow, the zone, that magical state where you perform almost effortlessly, totally focused, where time seems to slow down, and where you just enjoy being in the moment.

Just as you know when you're in the flow you also know when you're not. Often, when you're not, it's because you're trying.

> **PERFORMANCE TIP**
> *Challenge + Belief = Flow*

If you find yourself out of the flow, having to think about your flying, struggling to keep up, then it's important to concentrate on getting back into the flow and regaining your rhythm. A couple of minutes of talking yourself around the sky may help. Better yet, you can use a trigger word for a performance state of mind.

Performance Versus Results

Many pilots become too focused on the result of their flight test, simulator session or on what their competitors are doing in a flying competition. They're constantly worried about what the Examiner of Airmen is thinking, how their assessment is going or looking at what the competition is doing.

If they put that much focus and concentration on their flying, they would probably be so far ahead they would never have to worry about the result. You're going to be more successful if you concentrate on your performance rather than on the result or what other pilots are capable of, especially during flight tests, simulator sessions, or competition.

Concentrate and work on getting 100% out of yourself and your flying. Don't worry about the result; don't worry about the competition. If you're getting 100% out of yourself, there is not much else you can do about how an examiner is assessing your performance, or the competition, anyhow. If you don't pass, or you don't win, there is not much you can do other than improving your personal performance level; work at raising your personal 100%. After all, your 100% today may be only 90% six months from now because your technique has improved. You can always improve.

Consider competitive flying for a moment. By the very definition of the word "competitor," we compete against others. However, if your focus is on competing, you lessen your chances of performing well. The same holds true for flying tests. If you focus only on the result, what you have done well and what you haven't, you decrease your capacity to concentrate on what is important in the moment. When you focus on your performance (the act or task of flying), you increase your chances of performing well and, therefore, achieving your goals. Ironic, isn't it?

Focus on your performance, your execution, rather than the result. Paradoxically, your best results will come when you are least concerned with them - when you focus on your performance. This concept may be one of the most difficult "peak performance" concepts to accept. After all, flight tests and competitions are all about results. However, when you detach yourself from the results you will reduce your stress level, become more relaxed, your brain will be integrated, you will be "in the flow," and the results will take care of themselves.

If you think about it, you really can't control what the examiner is thinking or what your competition does. You have very little direct influence on them. All you can do is control your performance. So, focus on what you can control, not what you can't.

Of all the athletes Ross has coached over the years, it's the ones who are constantly looking at and comparing themselves to their competition that struggle the most. Athletes, and pilots, who focus on themselves and don't worry about anyone else are the ones who achieve most often.

Don't worry about what other people say and don't compare yourself to others. Judge or evaluate yourself based solely upon what you've done, your performance, not on what other people say or think. Compare yourself with your past performance, and strive to improve, no matter how you compare to the competition or other students. Do what you think is right for you to achieve the goals you've set for yourself. Only you know what is right for you.

Achievers focus on themselves today, in the present. They spend very little time, if any at all, looking at or talking about what they did or achieved in the past or what they will do in the future except for the sole purpose of getting themselves into a performance state of mind (e.g. replaying past successes). They look at the past only to learn from it and improve. They have short- and long-term goals, but they know it is today's performance that will enable them to achieve these goals.

Research has shown that athletes focused on their performance, their technique, have sharper vision and quicker reflexes than athletes focused on their results. It is when you totally focus on the task at hand, *in the present*, not on what has or will happen, that you most effectively activate your subconscious performance programs.

So, if removing the emphasis or focus from results and placing it strictly on the act of flying (your performance) is the best way to increase your chances of great results, does this mean that results are not important? Of course, they are! They matter very much. Think of all the flight tests you will need to do in your career. The objective is obviously to achieve a pass result.

Often in flying, whether for a test or competition, there is a desired result as the objective of a flight but the result should not be the focus. A great performance will guarantee the desired result. Use the strategies presented throughout this book to ensure you have great performances rather than crummy ones. If you do that, the results will look after themselves.

Pilots with an absolute burning desire to perform seem to have the knack of performing at their very best on a consistent basis. They are the ones who would do whatever it takes to perform. They spend the time preparing, physically and mentally, and they perform at their peak more often than anyone else. Their focus always seems to be on improving their performance, and the results just look after themselves.

Sometimes pilots have bad days. They make a mistake in a flight test, and they don't pass. Some pilots take a training failure harder than others. Unfortunately, this attitude often leads to more poor performances and more failures. Pilots who look at a failure as something to learn from, and obviously not something to enjoy or be satisfied with, are the ones who most often come back to perform well next time out.

Competitive people, people who want or need to feel they are above average, are the ones who most need to learn from their failures. If you become overly upset and focused on a failure, and never learn from it, you are bound to fail again and again.

So, here's a question for you: do you typically perform at your best when you're trying particularly hard or when you're relaxed? We're not suggesting that relaxed is not caring, being unfocused, or not performing at your maximum, but there is a huge difference between trying hard and being relaxed and focused.

> **PERFORMANCE TIP**
> *Focus on your performance and the results will look after themselves.*

Think back to some of your great performances in your life whether in a sport or anything else. Were you tense and aggressively trying, forcing yourself to perform well? Or were you relaxed, calm, focused, assertive, and simply doing what seemed to come naturally? We bet you were in the latter mode, not even aware that you trusted your subconscious programming to perform.

Again, focus on what you can control. Focus on what you want. Focus on where you want to go. Focus on the moment, your execution, your form, your technique, rather than on how much more of the flight there is to go, sequences you still need to complete, or how your assessment is going.

Expectations

Expectations - thinking about a competition result or test score - can limit your performance. With expectations, you focus on the outcome, the result, and that distracts you from the moment, your technique and ultimately your performance.

Expectations do not have any direction. It is like you saying, "I *expect* to go skiing in Colorado next year." That certainly doesn't get you to Colorado, does it? There is no plan, strategy or direction. If you say, "My *goal* is to go skiing in Colorado next year," it naturally leads you to develop a plan to get there.

If you expect a particular result, and it doesn't occur, you become frustrated or disappointed. Neither feeling helps get you any closer to the result you are seeking.

One of the flying instructors we spoke with said the following with regards to expectations, "I found that if a student was expecting just to scrape by in a flight test (for whatever reason), even if they were a very competent pilot, scraping by is generally all they ever did. They never surprised on the upside."

Expectations can also be limitations. Going into an aerobatic competition, for example, you think that given the current weather, if you score a 90% perfect score in each of your sequences, that will put you on the podium. You head into the air and score a 90%. What are the odds of you going much better in your subsequent sequences? Not good. After all, you matched your expectations. Consciously, you may not be satisfied with the score, but if you put a score into your subconscious, your mind will do what it takes to match it and not go beyond it. What if the wind conditions changed for the better? So, perhaps a 90% would have put you on the podium based on the pilots ahead of you, but drops you from the standings given the improved conditions for the pilots following you.

Expectations may also be a source of additional, unnecessary pressure in a testing scenario. Let's say you have been scheduled for your flight test or simulator renewal with a testing officer who has a reputation for being tough. This reputation may be true, or it may be a consequence of stories spread by embittered students who received a fail mark from the testing officer, but who fail to mention that they went to the test unprepared. Either way, why let expectations heap a load of extra, unnecessary pressure on yourself? Instead, shut the stories out (ignore any expectation of a tough time), be prepared as you would be in any testing situation, concentrate on your performance, and let the results take care of themselves.

Michael Jordan, one of the greatest athletes of all time, would recall images of past successes in high-pressure situations. As Jordan's Chicago Bulls coach Phil Jackson says in his book, *Sacred Hoops*, "Jordan doesn't believe in trying to visualize the shot in specific detail. 'I know what I want the outcome to be,' he says, 'but I don't try to see myself doing it beforehand. In 1982, I knew I wanted to make that shot [the last-second shot he used to take his University of North Carolina team to the NCAA Championship]. I didn't know where I was going shoot it or what kind of shot I was going to take. I just believed I could do it, and I did.'" That's open-ended imagery. That's having an empty mind, a beginner's mind - one without expectations.

Expectations are limitations, and you rarely exceed your expectations. Expectations program results into your mind, and your mind is very efficient at running those programs - sometimes too efficient! With expectations, you have pressure, stress, and anxiety that will negatively affect your performance. Plus, you will rarely ever exceed your expectations. Expectations can be dangerous things.

Possibilities and potentialities can be marvelous things. When you have no expectations, you have no limits and no preconceived ideas or thoughts

> **PERFORMANCE TIP**
> *Don't set expectations; focus on the possibilities and your potential.*

to un-focus your mind. If you focus on your goals, such as performing at your very best, you then have a direction to follow, one that will more likely lead to the desired result.

Pressure

It's quite frustrating to observe the pressure the media often places on young athletes. It's almost like they go around with a "can of pressure" and spray it all over the athletes, particularly during and leading up to the Olympic Games. The media seems to love to remind Olympic athletes of past failures and mistakes and ask them if they will be able to "put that out of their minds." If they truly cared about the performances of the Olympic athletes they wouldn't ask these types of questions. The same is true of our family, friends, work colleagues, and even ourselves. All can unwittingly pile added pressure on a pilot. For a pilot, having an understanding of and a strategy for controlling pressure is critical.

Their fear of failing limits many pilots' performance levels. So much of their focus is on "not failing" (an outcome) and what failing will mean (at least, what they think failing will mean) that they are almost guaranteed to fail. It's unfortunate, not to mention destructive, the amount of pressure (internal and external) some pilots put on themselves or have put on them by others.

For tasks with more than a simple degree of difficulty (e.g., flying), research has shown that there is a subtle relationship between pressure and performance. Up to a point, pressure has an energizing effect. Too little pressure (arousal) and we feel unchallenged and unmotivated and, subsequently, our performance is lackluster. Too much pressure (stress)

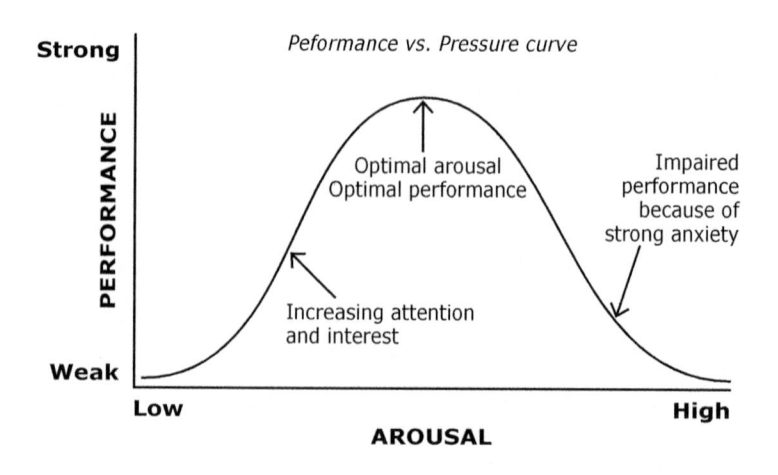

Peformance vs. Pressure curve

and we start to "fall apart." We are overwhelmed by demands or become task-saturated, and our cognitive processes (e.g., attention, memory and problem solving) are impaired. At a moderate level of pressure (neither too little arousal nor too much stress) we are "in the flow" and give our best performances. We are motivated to perform but not overwhelmed.

Internal pressure is not necessarily a bad thing as long as we focus it in the right direction. In fact, this sometimes helps to drive or motivate a person, but most of the time the pressure to deliver an outcome results only in increased tension, stress, and anxiety which decrease performance. Make sure you focus any internal pressure you place on yourself on your performance, not the result.

External pressure is what a pilot puts on themselves to perform in front of others or to live up to other's expectations. It's also the pressure others (family, friends, employers, managers, instructors or examiners) put on the pilot to perform. External pressure rarely, if ever, increases a pilot's performance level and most often negatively impacts performance.

People who place this external pressure on you most probably don't realize how much they can negatively affect you with their expectations. Understand that there is a difference between having and showing confidence in you and having high expectations. Having confidence is a performance-related thing. High expectations are result-orientated. Of course, you know which is best.

The same thing applies to you. If you think about what people expect of you, what they will say about you, what their expectations are, you decrease your chances of performing. If you focus on your performance and forget about whether you may fail and the consequences of that, you increase your chances of achieving your aims.

Choking

Consider the soccer player missing the penalty shot that costs his country the World Cup. He's made that shot hundreds, if not thousands, of times in practice. It's become completely automated, so why does he miss when it counts?

Evidence indicates that pressure resulting from wanting to do well causes us to focus our attention towards the conscious control over the execution of a movement. This conscious control disrupts the subconscious nature of the movement's execution resulting in an inferior performance. In other words, we choke!

When we learn a new motor task, we tend to talk ourselves through it. This internal dialogue activates the language centers in the left hemisphere of our brain. With repetition (practice), the motor task is programmed into a subconscious movement and the visual-spatial processes in the right hemisphere of our brain become dominant.

Conscious monitoring of the execution of a motor task brought about by the pressure of wanting to perform skillfully results in higher left hemisphere activation. In effect, we reactivate our language centers as we would when first learning a task as opposed to letting the program just run from our subconscious. Disruption of the automatic execution of a skilled behavior results in an inferior performance.

Research by sports psychologists has shown that a skilled performance under pressure requires either reduced left hemisphere activity or enhanced right hemisphere activity. But how do we facilitate this?

An activity that activates one hemisphere of the brain creates an advantage for the performance of activities that rely on that hemisphere. Our upper limbs connect with the cross-lateral brain hemispheres, and extensive research has shown that by clenching your left fist for just 30 seconds at a time causes the right hemisphere of your brain to be activated.

So, to prime yourself for peak performance you should squeeze your left hand before performing a task under pressure as part of your pre-performance routine along with the mental imagery, PPT, and trigger word tools we have already mentioned.

Belief System

At one time, scientists, researchers, and athletes thought that if someone were to run the mile in less than four minutes, they would practically drop dead. Then, in 1954, along came Roger Bannister who didn't believe these "laws of physics" and ran the first sub-four-minute mile. Within the following twelve months, four other runners ran a sub-four-minute mile, a limit that for decades had seemed impossible. Once armed with the knowledge - with the belief - that it was doable, it was relatively easy.

The power of your belief system is amazing. Our world, especially the world of sports and physical pursuits, has countless examples of the power of the belief system. This fact has been proven time and time again by world champions and amateurs alike. Watch any world champion, and you can't help being impressed with more than their skills. It is the strength of their belief system, on a consistent basis, that is most impressive and what makes them as successful as they are.

Do you think that Tiger Woods consistently had stronger self-belief than his competitors when he set the record for the number of weeks leading the world golf rankings? What about Roger Federer? Do you think that he consistently had stronger self-belief than his competitors when he set the record for the number of weeks leading the world tennis rankings? There's no doubt about it. You could hear it in the words of their competitors: they talked about having to beat Tiger or Roger, whereas Tiger or Roger mostly talked about themselves and their performance. What about the belief Lee Westwood must have had in himself to replace Tiger Woods as the number one golfer in the world after a record 281 weeks? You know that he must have known he could beat Tiger. Likewise, Rafael Nadal must have believed that he was every bit as good as, or better than, Roger Federer to displace him after 237 weeks at the top of the ATP rankings. In all these athletes, you can see it in their walk, you can see it in their eyes, you can hear it in their words, and you can see it on the court or links.

So, how is our belief system developed? How does one develop a set of beliefs that are as strong as a world champion's, a world's number one? Where do a pilot's beliefs originate? We program our subconscious belief system in three different ways:

- Physically/Experientially
- Mentally
- Externally/Internally

Physical/Experiential Programming

We're sure you've witnessed this yourself many times. A pilot who seems to have all the aptitude and training to be a great pilot just doesn't seem to get it together to perform when the pressure is on. Then, practically out of the blue, they have a great flight, score very well in a flight test, simulator session or a competition and look out! They begin to perform at that level consistently or win every competition in sight. What was the difference? Did they gain a bunch of flying talent all of a sudden? No, just one thing changed: their belief system.

Earlier in the book, we talked about a season where Ross was racing and was extremely successful over the first lap or two, gaining at least three or four positions on the first lap of every race. As that season wore on, he developed a very strong belief that he was the fastest starter.

When you experience being on top of your game, your belief system is programmed to believe you are a proficient pilot. Conversely, if you are struggling with accuracy, you will form a belief that you're not a proficient pilot. This method of programming is how most of your belief system develops.

If you honestly believe deep down inside that you have a special knack for avoiding the common errors made by others, the odds are that you will. The reverse is also true. It is almost a self-fulfilling prophecy. If you make the same error over a couple of flights and begin to believe that you have a competency issue, the chances are that you will start to talk yourself into repeating the error and reinforcing the pattern. Through your belief system, you are programming the error and increasing the probability of repeating it.

On the other hand, if you are continually avoiding the same errors and putting in a series of solid performances, you begin to think that maybe you are good at avoiding issues with your flying. You continue to have success, and that reinforces your belief system. Now you know you are good and, because of that, you are.

Often, a pilot's beliefs about their abilities and prowess come before they ever sit in the control seat of an aircraft. If you have been successful in other areas of your life, particularly other sports or physical skills, you begin to believe that you are good at many things. The more success you have had in other areas, the stronger your beliefs will be.

Mental Programming

Most of the programming of your beliefs comes about from past experiences, but what if you've never done something in the past such as blitzing a test or winning a competition? How can you begin to believe that you can? Which comes first, the belief of being capable or truly being capable which results in the belief of being capable? How can you begin to believe you're competent before you are?

The solution to the problem of developing a belief in being able to do something before you've experienced it is all in your mind. By pre-playing being proficient in your mind, using mental imagery, you can develop a belief in being able to do it.

Right now, for a few minutes, imagine being in your aircraft ready for your next flight test, aerobatic competition, or whatever part of your flying gives you the opportunity to show off what you can do. Imagine as many of the details as possible: other traffic, the surrounding terrain, weather, sounds, the examiner, everything.

PERFORMANCE TIP
What you believe is what you get.

Now, see yourself shutting down or sitting at the debriefing. Stop reading and do this.

Now, go back to your image of you about to start your flight test or competition and then sitting at the debriefing. How did you score? If you imagine yourself in any situation other than having been entirely successful, the likelihood of being entirely successful is small. If you can't believe you can do something, it's less likely that you will be able to do it. Until you can imagine yourself scoring a near perfect score, to do it would almost be a fluke. In other words, until you believe you can, it's unlikely that you will.

Your mind, or should we say the use of your mind in a deliberate, productive manner, can shape reality. In other words, what you believe and what you mentally "see" can come true (become reality) if you focus on it.

External/Internal Programming

Your belief system - what you believe about yourself - plays a critical role in your flying performance. In fact, what you believe about yourself, your deep-seated inner confidence, will have more of a bearing on your performance than just about anything else.

You and other people can have a significant effect on your belief system. If someone were to tell you continually that you're a great pilot, over time, you could begin to believe that you're a great pilot. Of course, the opposite is also true.

Your self-talk can also affect your beliefs. The more times you repeat a phrase, the more it will become a part of your belief system. If you tell yourself over and over again that you are a great instrument pilot, you will eventually truly believe you are a great instrument pilot, and the greater your chances are of being just that. If you keep telling yourself that you're not proficient, it will have a negative effect. It is a self-fulfilling prophecy.

> **PERFORMANCE TIP**
> *Whether you believe you can or believe you can't, either way you're correct.*

The bottom line is if you do not believe you're a great pilot, you never will be. What you believe about yourself is the single biggest limitation to your performance.

Changing Your Beliefs

The good news is that you can change your beliefs about yourself. The first step in changing your belief system is getting an awareness of just what your beliefs are. You should make a list of both your positive and negative beliefs, being totally honest with yourself. The list should include what you believe about yourself from both the physical technique aspect and the mental side. You do not need to share the list with anyone else. This list only serves for you to become more aware of yourself. After all, if you don't know what to change, how are you going to change it?

Once you're honestly aware of what your beliefs are, you can choose to reprogram any negative ones. That will rarely happen overnight. It usually requires doing a couple of mental imagery sessions per day, backing that up with some physical signs of improvement, more mental programming, more physical evidence and programming, and so on. Without the mental programming, it is unlikely your beliefs will ever change unless by some fluke you happen to improve, in which case you will have experienced it.

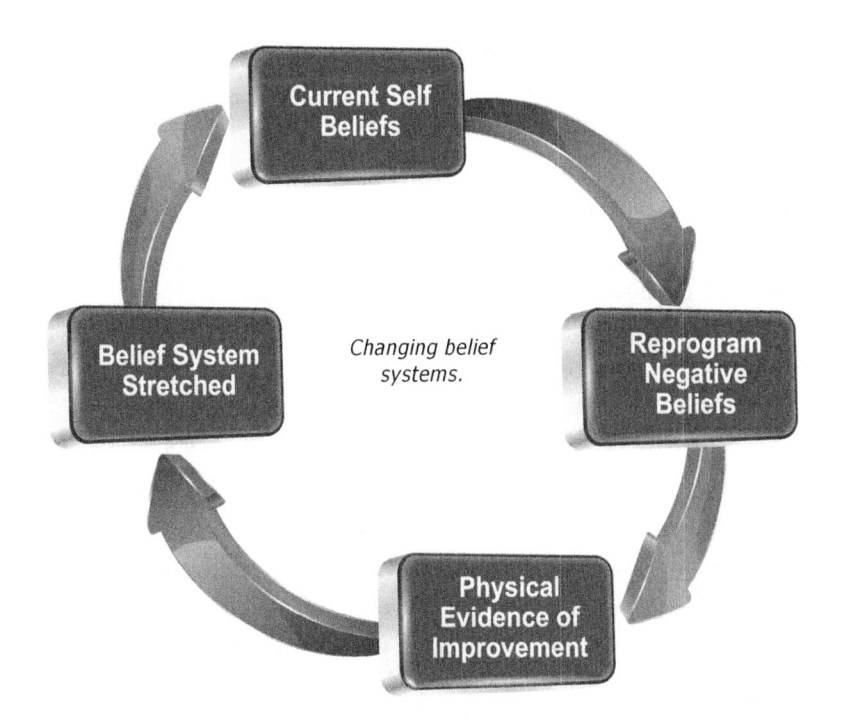

Changing belief systems.

Let's assume for a minute that you've never scored above average in a test or competition. If you begin doing mental imagery of great performances and see yourself now being above average, will that change your beliefs enough to enable you to achieve the perfect score the next time out? Maybe it will; maybe it won't. The problem is that your mind (your current belief system) may not accept that much of an improvement. You know... you may be able to fool other people, but you can't fool yourself.

Your belief system is a bit like an elastic band. You can stretch it, but if you stretch it too much, it can snap. Seeing yourself moving from average to "God's gift to aviation" in one flight may be too much of a stretch; your belief system will then snap, and you won't accept it.

> **PERFORMANCE TIP**
>
> *Stretch your belief system, bit by bit, through self-talk and mental programming.*

An effective way to stretch your belief system is to have a reason for stretching it. If you've not made any changes in your skills or your approach, it's difficult to see why you should change your beliefs. However, if you've learned something new and put in place some strategies like those outlined in this book, then there is a reason for your belief to stretch.

The strategies, triggers, actions, centering and integration exercises presented in this book work in two ways. First, they physiologically and psychologically "switch you on." Secondly, if you believe they will help you perform better, they will. That is the power of the belief system.

Having a reason to stretch your belief system is also one reason coaches for aerobatic pilots can help so much. While a good coach will help improve your technique and mental preparation, often a big reason for the improvement is that your belief system can accept there is a reason for improvement. If you believe you can or should improve, you will improve. By simply having a coach, a new set of mental strategies, or whatever, there's a reason for your belief system to accept a stretch from average to excellence.

A powerful technique for replacing bad self-beliefs you may hold about your capabilities with positive self-beliefs is the contrary evidence technique. With the contrary evidence technique, you need to take the negative self-belief and look for as many pieces (at least ten) of evidence or examples from your past that you can think of that contradict that negative belief. Then, when you find yourself falling back on your negative self-beliefs, you can replay your examples of contrary evidence to dissuade yourself of these beliefs.

Let's use the example of the pilot who doubts their ability to handle abnormal, non-normal, or emergency situations or doesn't believe they can perform well in stressful conditions. The contrary evidence they could use would include specific examples of stressful situations they have handled well in the past, practice sessions where they coped well with complex simulated emergencies, important flight tests that ended in a great result, etc.

If you truly want to change your beliefs, the best method of all would be a combination of the contrary evidence technique, mental programming, positive self-talk, and giving yourself a reason to accept the stretched belief.

> **PERFORMANCE TIP**
> *Use your strengths to program over the top of weaknesses.*

Let's consider the pilot who feels they start simulator sessions well but loses the edge approaching the end; they finish weak. This self-belief that they can't sustain their performance level over the duration of a session leaves them very confident and proficient at the start of the session; they are so busy concentrating on getting everything right that they don't have time to lose confidence and therefore they don't make mistakes. As the session progresses, and they have time to think, they start to anticipate a degradation in their performance, and they lose confidence. As their confidence or belief in themselves fades, so does their performance.

It's no use telling this pilot they should stop thinking that way. Telling a pilot who is not confident to be more confident is like telling a depressed person to be happy. That just doesn't work. Until this pilot changes their mental programming, the kind of change they need isn't going to happen.

So, how do they counter this thinking? How does a strong starter who feels that they fade finish strong? How do they sustain a level of performance throughout a flight or simulator session?

Starting with the contrary evidence method, they may find that there are plenty of examples to contradict the self-belief that they lose the edge as time progresses through a flight. These examples can be from anywhere: simulator sessions where they have performed strongly throughout or had a great final sequence, long flights through the night when they have pulled off a fantastic landing in inclement conditions, achieving a great score in the last flight of a long weekend aerobatic competition, etc.

Using any example the pilot can think of that supports the alternative argument - that they *are* a strong finisher and that they *can* maintain performance levels over the duration of a flight test - can be used in mental imagery sessions to program over the contrary, negative belief.

Because they know they are good at the start of a session, they could also use mental imagery to prepare for their simulator session, treating each and every sequence with the same mindset as if it is the start of a session.

This pilot's mental imagery programming would consist of flying each sequence in turn, resetting between each sequence to refresh their mental imagery, and seeing, feeling, and hearing every detail of the sensations they experience at the start of a session when their confidence is highest. They would feel the emotions of flying those first sequences and the associated state of mind. They could even mix up the order of the sequences to be flown in the simulator so that the sequences to be flown at the end of the simulator session were, in fact, the opening sequences in their mental imagery session. Doing this over and over again in their mind creates a confident, assured self-image for flying all the sequences, no matter when they fly them within the simulator session.

Repeating these mental imagery sessions in the weeks leading up to the simulator session, every time our example pilot begins a new sequence they would also provide themselves a trigger word to reset this mindset of the confidence they already have at the start of a simulator session. At any time during the session, they could use something like, "begin again," "reset," or "first sequence" to trigger a pre-existing mental program for the confident feelings they previously associated with the beginning of a simulator session.

As time progresses, the pilot should find that they *can* sustain a level of performance over a longer period. Not only does this give them more examples to feed back into their contrary evidence work and mental imagery sessions but the actual physical improvement (combined with the application of the strategies) gives solid reasons to stretch their belief system to accept that they are a strong finisher after all.

The Inner Game of Flying

This final chapter on mental aspects of flying looks at philosophical or attitudinal approaches to peak performance flying. Some of the concepts introduced tie together information and concepts from preceding chapters.

Comfort Zone

For the vast majority of pilots, most of their flying will be well within the structural and performance limits of the aircraft they fly and will, therefore, be well within the comfort zone of the experienced operator. There are, however, numerous situations that may cause you to feel uncomfortable at the controls.

There are many times when optimized performance (aircraft or personal) is required; well within the aircraft limits but that are taxing on the pilot and can stretch their comfort levels. If you are unfamiliar with the equipment you're operating, time is critical, a complex operation requires task prioritization, it is crucial to optimize the aircraft performance or fly at the edge of its envelope, then you may very well find yourself operating at the very edges of your comfort zone.

When you are unfamiliar with the aircraft type you are flying or a more complex operational environment, it can sometimes feel as if everything is happening very quickly. In fact, it's almost as if you can't keep up or don't have time to think. You almost feel as if you are trying to hold on to the horizontal stabilizer as the aircraft rockets away from you! With experience, your comfort zone expands as you become more comfortable with and accustomed to the speed and feel of the aircraft and you consequently feel confident flying in your new aircraft type or role.

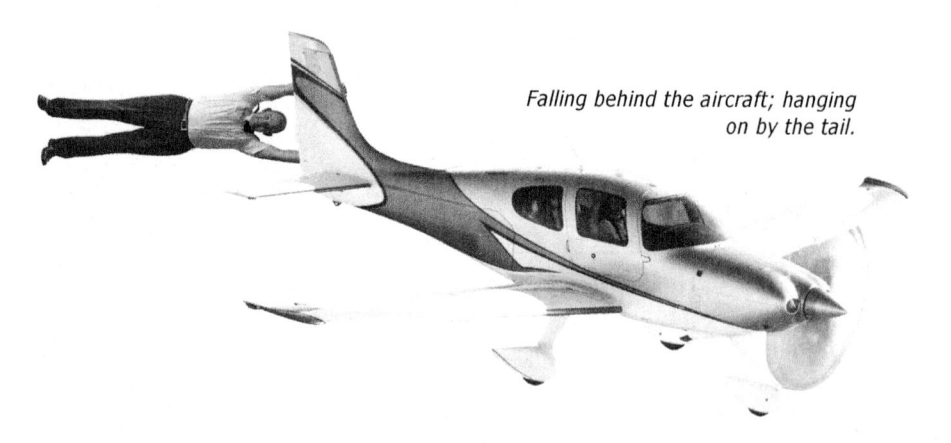

Falling behind the aircraft; hanging on by the tail.

Some pilots adapt more quickly than others to faster aircraft, a change of seat, or a new role. This adaptability doesn't necessarily mean they are better pilots, just that they can expand the limits of their comfort zone more quickly. So what can we do to stretch our comfort zone?

Firstly, if it's a case of you feeling as though things are happening too fast, as though you're rushing, it may just mean you're not looking or thinking far enough ahead. Being able to manage higher performance aircraft does not require thinking faster (we can only think at one speed), it requires thinking further ahead and anticipating. As an extreme example, the SR-71 had a minimum turning radius at altitude of about 80 nautical miles. If an SR-71 pilot waited until over a waypoint to begin a turn onto their next track, they would be creating work for themselves fixing the resulting track error on the next leg. Pick up your vision, or anticipate earlier, and your comfort zone will expand.

If you feel uncomfortable or lose confidence when loaded up or task-saturated, another way to stretch your comfort zone is to fly an aircraft that is more capable or complex than the one you normally operate (obviously this won't always be practical). You could also take on duties beyond your normal role under the supervision of an instructor or safety pilot. By becoming accustomed to being loaded up, when you return to a normal workload it feels easy. The true objective is to help delay the point at which you begin to feel overloaded.

Short of spending time behind the controls of an aircraft much more capable or complex than yours, mental imagery is the best avenue for developing your comfort zone (it's a lot cheaper too!). One way this can be done is by flying very complex scenarios in your mind or adding additional tasks to your workload.

To be better, to improve as a pilot, or to be able to readily optimize the operation of your aircraft, your comfort zone will need to extend to at least the limits of your aircraft. In other words, if you are not comfortable flying the aircraft close to its operational limits (e.g., at maximum crosswind, maximum take-off weight, short strips) you will not be able to maximize your performance or fully utilize the aircraft. If we can stretch our comfort zone to at least encompass the operational envelope of the aircraft we fly, we can minimize the chances of finding ourselves in uncomfortable situations.

To expand our performance limits takes experience and constantly pushing the limits of your comfort zone. When we are talking about optimizing the performance of the aircraft, however, or operating it at its performance limits, we are talking in finites. There is no stretching to be had. The limits are limits, they are there for our safety, and we can't breach them. However, there are many situations that will require us to optimize aircraft performance within very fine margins or even approach operational limits. The importance of precision when operating at the edges of the performance or operational envelope can bring with it a whole new level of anxiety and stress but, once again, there are ways we can expand our comfort zone so that we can be comfortable in these scenarios.

If you are a fighter or aerobatic pilot, you will no doubt sometimes push your aircraft to the very edge of its performance limits. Pilots familiar with operating on the edge of the stall or minimizing turn radius know that optimized flying at the performance limits means that sometimes you will exceed those limits, fall out of a maneuver or not have the aircraft performing optimally. For example, to fly a minimum radius turn, to get the g-load and speed exactly right, it's a matter of flying a little over, under, over, under, over, until you average out being right at the very knife edge of optimized performance. Sure, you need to be smooth and tidy, but there are times when you can take that approach a little too far. If, for example, you have never pushed the aircraft deep into the buffet until you have stalled, how do you know how close to the limit you are?

> **PERFORMANCE TIP**
> *If you need to optimize performance, explore the aircraft's behavior.*

If the type of flying you do (e.g., aerobatics or air combat maneuvering) necessitates you flying right up to an actual structural limitation, the importance of not exceeding those limits may be a cause of significant discomfort. Discomfort can cause us to stiffen up and this, in turn, inhibits real finesse on the controls right when finesse and a deft touch is precisely what is required. Some pilots understand that there may be a certain level of discomfort (or stress) when operating towards an aircraft limit, but they are uncomfortable with that. It's like they know they need to be on that ragged edge but they don't feel at home there.

Consider that the mental image you may need is of being slightly uncomfortable, but (and this is important) being comfortable being uncomfortable. Use mental imagery of other situations where you've not felt comfortable in the past. Replay anything that felt uncomfortable in the past and feel your comfort level matching it. Then see your comfort "envelope" stretching with everything you did feeling more and more comfortable. See yourself craving a little bit of uncomfortableness. Feel your body tingle with that uncomfortable feeling but still breathing normally and getting a big kick out of the feeling.

> **PERFORMANCE TIP**
> *Be comfortable being uncomfortable.*

Part of being comfortable is being prepared and ready for any condition or situation. For many pilots, the sight of the windsock rigidly at right angles to the runway sends them into a fit of nervousness and undermines their confidence. They "know" they *are not* good in a crosswind and therefore they are not good in a crosswind. Other pilots get a big grin at even the thought of it beginning to blow. It's related to being comfortable being uncomfortable. But part of it is just feeling ready, which is another thing for which you can use mental imagery.

See, feel, and hear yourself being competent in all the tough stuff. Build a program for feeling comfortable when you're uncomfortable and know that when you're uncomfortable, other pilots are also uncomfortable. The difference is you're ready for it; you've prepared, and therefore you're comfortable being uncomfortable.

The best pilots love any condition or situation. It's as if they get better when the conditions are worse; the tougher and more demanding the conditions, the more at home they are. They get to demonstrate to themselves that they are great pilots. You want to be comfortable being uncomfortable, no matter the conditions.

> **PERFORMANCE TIP**
> *Be prepared by preparing mentally.*

Apart from the use of mental imagery, the next step in stretching your comfort zone is to do so with an experienced instructor. You can still feel uncomfortable and push the limits, but you know that you'll be safe as the instructor is there to make sure of that. If you go out and explore the limits of your airplane alone, then you may be setting up for disaster. Lots of pilots have killed themselves trying to teach themselves aerobatics or trying new things without having had the proper training or experience. Being uncomfortable is fine as long as it's very carefully managed and, most preferably, with an experienced instructor with you.

To improve your performance level - to stretch the limits of your comfort zone - you have to push your limits in small increments, progressively. Some pilots never go beyond their comfort zone and never improve. Others go too far, too soon. If you take too big a leap, at best, you won't improve. At worst, you will exceed an aircraft limit or crash!

If you are exploring your limits on your own, make sure you leave room for error. For example, say you are going out to practice spinning in a single-seater aerobatic aircraft for the first time. You may have a low-level aerobatic endorsement, but why start out spinning to your limits? Consider starting out with a "pull out or bail out" limit: e.g., "If I lose control and have not recovered by 3,000 feet, I'm parachuting out." If you start feeling uncomfortable, listen to the little voice and don't ignore the hairs on the back of your neck standing up. Back off, or knock off, the drill until you've established why you are uncomfortable. Sometimes being uncomfortable, but listening to that little voice and responding, keeps us safe.

Confidence

Confidence builds success and successes build confidence. It's a loop. The more confidence you have, the more likely you will have success. The more success you have, the more confidence you will have. Unfortunately, the opposite is also true!

Setting and achieving short-term and long-term goals is important to your confidence. To achieve goals, they must be realistic. Do not try to progress too quickly. If you get behind the controls of an aircraft and attempt maneuvers that you are neither mentally nor physically ready for, it's very easy for you to lose confidence.

For example, say you are looking at improving your altitude control while flying a steep turn. If your immediate goal is to maintain altitude within plus or minus 200 feet (as required for a flight test), that's achievable and helps build confidence so that you can improve even more. It may be too large a jump if your immediate goal is to hold altitude within 50ft. If you don't succeed in making that jump, you may lose confidence and not make any further improvement.

Have you ever noticed how you could "see" a person's confidence level? It's interesting how you can often notice how strong a belief a person has in him or herself, especially in sport. You can watch pilots walk to their aircraft and often get a feeling which one is a great pilot. For example, you never see Red Bull Air Race pilots casually stroll to their aircraft, looking like they don't care, don't mean business, or don't believe deep down inside that they're going to win, and then go out and win. Pilots who consistently win look like they're going to win. You can "see" the belief in their eyes and their walk.

No doubt you will have noticed this yourself, how some pilots just look like they are there to perform, and others do not. Most of that is in the way they present themselves, the way they walk. Another technique that can be used by pilots is to walk to their aircraft like they imagine a peak performance pilot would. In other words, act like a Chuck Yeager, a Neil Armstrong or a Charles Kingsford-Smith. If you model your walk after a pilot whose performances you would like to emulate, your state of mind cannot help but be closer to ideal. Used in conjunction with relating a previous positive experience, it is an extremely effective tool.

Fear

If anyone ever tells you they have never experienced fear when flying an aircraft, they are either lying or have never flown near the aircraft's limits. There's not a successful pilot in the world who hasn't scared themselves one time or another. No doubt about it, flying can be a risky endeavor. You need to plan to deal with the risks. As the saying goes, "If you fail to plan, you plan to fail." Fear, or at least self-preservation, is the only thing that stops you from taking the aircraft to places it just wasn't designed to go. On the other hand, if it's the kind of fear that makes you panic and "freeze up," then that's not good.

Fear comes in many forms, good and bad, or more accurately, useful and useless. The fear of physical injury resulting from a crash usually limits you from doing something stupid with the aircraft. We prefer to look at that as self-preservation, which is a good thing.

Conversely, some pilots want to achieve something but are too afraid of it not working out. Fear and desire are usually the opposite sides of the same coin. They focus on the fear of failure (a result) rather than the desire to make it work. When faced with a flight test or a difficult career decision, they think about what may happen if they make a mistake.

Fear can be debilitating. The fear of failure produces tension which disintegrates your brain, slows reflexes, and usually hurts your performance level. Of course, that usually produces the result you feared most. If you concentrate instead on your performance, rather than the problem or the result, fear of failure disappears. If you keep a clear mental picture of what you want to achieve, your mind will find a way of making it happen.

Keep in mind how valuable feedback and awareness are to learning and improving your performance. Success and failure are simply the results of doing something. Failure is just a result you didn't want, one that you can learn from and help you improve your performance. Use failure as feedback on what corrections are required to guide you towards your objective.

If you are fearful of some aspect of flying, be it practicing forced landings, an aerobatic maneuver, or some aspect of airline flying, talk to a more experienced pilot you respect (a mentor). Talk through what you're worried about and get some perspective as to whether it's a real and sensible fear that you should respect or if it's unfounded. If it's the latter, use this knowledge to develop a strategy to overcome the fear using mental imagery and the strategies we've outlined for changing belief systems.

Another way of dealing with fear is to implement a strategy to restore calm by training your ability to shift emotions via mental imagery. Try this exercise. Close your eyes and visualize fear. Physically, how does fear feel? Now visualize calmness. Physically, how does calm feel? Notice everything you can about how calm feels.

By using mental imagery sessions to practice recreating the feeling of calm, you should be able to move into a calm state whenever you need to by recreating the physiology of calm. A trigger word enhances this ability. This strategy is not just limited to dealing with fear, though.

It can be used to learn how to move seamlessly from any negative or unwanted emotion to a more desirable or wanted emotion.

Motivation

If you want to succeed, if you want to perform, you must be motivated. No one, no matter how much talent they have, will ever be a consistent performer if they lack motivation. If you want to perform, you have to be "hungry." You have to want it more than anything else.

It's important to identify for yourself why you want to be a pilot and then ask yourself, do you want to be a great pilot? What is it about flying that you enjoy? Be honest. It doesn't matter what it is. What does matter is that once you've identified it, you should *focus* on it. To be motivated, you must love what you are doing. Remember and relive what you love about flying. If that doesn't motivate you, nothing will.

If you are not 100% motivated, it is doubtful you will perform consistently at 100%. Focus on what you truly enjoy or love about flying. Motivation mostly comes from the love of what you're doing. As part of your regular mental imagery sessions see yourself enjoying the art of flying, experiencing the thrill of flying, loving every second of it!

Moderation can in fact help increase your motivation level. Taking a break from flying to the point where you miss it may be just what the motivation doctor ordered. Because it costs so much to get more flying hours in your log book, most pilots do not have to worry about flying too often!

Flying can be such an all-encompassing passion that many pilots spend practically 24 hours a day, seven days a week eating, breathing, and living flying. If that is you, when you finally get behind the controls of your aircraft some of the passion and burning desire to fly may be gone.

Keep your flying in perspective and a balance in your life. Remember why you fly. Do not take yourself, your career or your flying too seriously. Have fun. After all, that is why you started flying, wasn't it? You may have to remind yourself of that now and then!

Having said that, it is your level of commitment and burning desire that will determine more than anything else how well you perform and how far you go career-wise in professional flying (if that is your goal).

Much of your motivation comes from your expectations as to how you will do. If you believe you will not do well, most likely your motivation to do what is necessary to maximize your performance will not be there. Of course, this leads to a self-fulfilling prophecy.

> **PERFORMANCE TIP**
> *Focus on what you love about flying.*

You don't expect to do well, so you don't prepare, which leads to poor performance, which leads to a poor result, which meets your expectations.

Again, this is why it is so important to focus on your performance and not the result. There is never any reason you cannot perform at your maximum so there should never be any reason to become demotivated.

Having goals or objectives before each flight can certainly affect your motivation. Positive, achievable, challenging, performance-related goals give you something to strive for, something to go after. Conversely, unrealistic or easily-achieved goals will most likely discourage and demotivate you.

Perseverance, Commitment & Dedication

Did you know that Michael Jordan's high school varsity basketball team originally told him he wasn't good enough to play for them? Of course, we all know he didn't take that evaluation and walk away from the sport. Instead, he practiced every day until he made the team and the rest is history. The point is that he persevered and never gave up.

To be a great pilot takes a tremendous amount of work, sacrifice, commitment, perseverance, and dedication. Don't ever fool yourself - no matter how much talent you have, you will never be a top performer without those elements.

Commitment and perseverance alone will not guarantee success, but without them, you can guarantee you won't perform to your maximum. Sure, there have been many pilots who have made huge commitments, who have persevered, who have made the sacrifices, and who have not made it to the top. However, we also know of no pilot who has made it who hasn't made the commitment, who hasn't sacrificed and persevered.

The Final Word on the Inner Game

In all your mental imagery, see yourself in and out of the aircraft as relaxed and calm. If you fly competitively, see yourself focused on performing at your maximum and not particularly concerned with your competition. See yourself completely comfortable in your surroundings out of the aircraft and with the performance level of the aircraft. See yourself confident in your ability to perform. See your ideal level of "upness," not too psyched, intense or energized, but not too laid back, either. See yourself as assertive and making "smart" flying decisions. See yourself flying for the pure love of it, fully motivated to do whatever it takes to perform well. See yourself as fully prepared. You've eaten well; you've physically and mentally trained;

you're ready. See yourself facing some adversity but overcoming it by persevering, demonstrating your commitment to yourself and others. See yourself dealing with external pressure by focusing on your performance and letting that performance take care of the results.

Program all these feelings, these attitudes, states of mind, beliefs - relaxed but intense. Calm but energized. Psyched-up but in control. Focused but aware.

See, hear, and feel yourself performing better than you ever have and notice the result, something you want more than anything else in the world, but knowing it was your performance that produced the result.

Write down on a piece of paper what success in flying means to you. What do you want to achieve? How do you want to feel? For some pilots, becoming World Aerobatic Champion is the only objective. For others, it's to get paid to fly, no matter what type or level. Others still only want to fly for the pure enjoyment of it and whether they fly at an amateur level or make it a profession doesn't matter.

Then write down why you want to achieve that level of success. Is it to make lots of money, have lots of fame, feel good about yourself, for the sense of accomplishment, to fulfill the dreams of a parent, for the thrill of controlling an aircraft, to win competitions, or because you haven't found anything else at which you are truly proficient?

The point is, the reason doesn't matter. One reason is not any better than another. The key is to know why, for your own personal motivation. The more honest you are with yourself, the more effective this information will be to your motivation level. When you need that little "pick-me-up," focus on your ideal level of success and the reasons you want them to come to fruition.

As we mentioned, success (and feelings of success), leads to further success. Take some time to recall and write down at least three of the best performances of your life. These do not have to have anything to do with flying or have resulted in a victory or high grade. They can be how you performed in school, in another sport, something you accomplished in a job, or about a relationship. Make a note of how you felt before, during, and after these performances. Recall every detail you can about them. Relive them and write them down. Then, go back and read them now and then or update them with new experiences.

Pilot As Athlete

Is a pilot an athlete? At the end of the day, who cares? It takes great physical skill and endurance to fly an aircraft well, not to mention the mental demands. If you want to be even the slightest bit successful in flying, you need to be in good physical condition. If you want to make flying your profession, it helps to be in very good condition.

Physical Fitness

Flying fighter or aerobatic aircraft at the limit of their envelopes requires aerobic fitness, muscle strength, flexibility, and proper nutritional habits. Without these, you will lack the strength and endurance to not only be successful but also to fly safely. Using the controls and dealing with the tremendous g-forces on your body demands a great deal more than most people think, especially with the extreme heat you may have to work in wearing helmets, g-suits, parachutes, or other safety equipment.

To qualify for your flying license (and every year or two after that, depending on the level of license you have), you must have a full physical examination completed by your doctor. But even though you may be healthy according to a doctor, how physically fit are you? How strong? How supple and flexible?

When your body tires during a flight, it affects not only your physical abilities but also your mental abilities. When you physically tire and begin to notice aches and pains, or even before you notice them, it distracts your mind from what it should be doing: concentrating on flying.

The better conditioned your body, the more mentally alert you will be and the more effectively you'll be able to deal with stress and concentrate. A big part of the drain on your strength is the very intense and never-ending concentration you must maintain. Just a slight lapse in concentration can bring disaster. How many times have you heard the expression "brain fade" used as an excuse?

Have you ever noticed how often your own, or another pilot's, performance begins to progressively deteriorate near the end of a flight or simulator session as fatigue develops? Pilots who claim to stay in shape simply by flying are only fooling themselves. The workout you get from flying, even on a daily basis, is not good enough. You must supplement that with a regular physical conditioning program.

When you train, you become fitter. Stressing your body, in a controlled manner, through running, lifting weights, or other forms of exercise, gradually breaks down the muscle fiber. Then, with rest, the muscles heal stronger. So, each time you exercise, then rest, your body becomes stronger.

Use a regular fitness training program to improve your coordination, strength, flexibility, and endurance. Sports like running, tennis, racquetball, and squash are excellent for improving your cardiovascular fitness, coordination, and reflexes. Most of these will also improve your reaction skills. Adding specially-designed weight training, stretching, and foam-rolling programs to these activities could mean the difference between reaching peak performance and not.

Strength, particularly in high g-limited aircraft, is very important. So, weight training is key. Keep in mind; you don't want to bulk up too much if your cockpit tends to be very cramped. Concentrate on building muscle endurance as much as outright strength.

You should by now understand how critical it is to be sensitive to what the aircraft is telling you and to be precise in your use of the controls. To reinforce it, try this test. Trace over a picture with a pencil very accurately and with great detail. Then do 50 push-ups. Try tracing the picture again. What happened? When the muscles in your arms tire, you lose some of the precise control. You need that precise control when flying an aircraft.

During some forms of flying (aerobatics, air racing, fighter pilots), your cardiovascular system may take a real workout. The average person's heart rate at rest is between 50 and 80 beats per minute (BPM), less than half its maximum potential. Most athletes operate during their sport at around 60 to 70% of their maximum only for a few minutes at a time between rests. When straining against large g-forces, you may very well anticipate operating at close to 80% of your maximum BPM for the entire length of combat maneuvers or an aerobatic sequence.

Being aerobically fit, then, will make a difference to your performance. The only way to ensure your cardiovascular system is in shape is through aerobic training: running, cycling, Stairmaster, or any sport where you keep your heart rate at 60 to 70% of its maximum for at least 20 minutes and preferably more.

You can develop your reflexes. Sports such as squash, racquetball, and table tennis are great for improving your hand-eye coordination and reflexes. Computer and video games are also good for improving your mental processing and reflexes.

There are also benefits to be had by improving your flexibility. Fewer muscle aches and much less cramping while flying can only enhance your performance by eliminating a major source of distraction.

How's your weight? If you are overweight, you owe it to yourself to lose weight, especially if you are involved in sport aviation and can gain an advantage by getting airborne in a lighter aircraft. Why work at making your aircraft as light as possible if you're not, as well? Excess fat on your body works as insulation, something you don't need if your cockpit is a high-heat environment. Reducing your body fat content (or maintaining it if you're already lean enough) should be a part of your training program.

Dehydration can be one of a pilot's worst enemies. Dehydration can lead to weakened and cramping muscles and less effective mental processing. In fact, studies have shown that losing just two-percent of your body weight in sweat can reduce your work capacity by as much as 15%. There is only one solution for dehydration: drink fluids. Bear this in mind if hot environmental conditions, a requirement to wear fire-resistant clothing, continuous physical exertion or heat generated by the intrinsic nature of the aircraft type you fly makes for a less-than-ideal working environment.

> **PERFORMANCE TIP**
> *If you want to perform at your absolute peak, you owe it to yourself to be as physically fit as possible.*

It is a well-known fact that an athlete's diet is extremely important to their performance. Athletes from all fields are known to tailor their diets to the specific needs of their sports with both nutrition and hydration plans for training and competing. A pilot is no different. If you want to perform at your peak, follow a proper diet. Talk to a doctor or certified nutritionist.

Finally, do you drink much? How about smoking? We all know that alcohol and cigarettes affect your health. Even if there is a one-in-a-million chance that they could slow your reactions, affect your vision, or decrease your cardiovascular level, consider whether you want to take that chance. How committed are you to operating at your peak?

The effects of alcohol on your body and mind can last for a long time. It slows your reaction time, dulls your senses, and slows your ability to make decisions. Taking drugs to improve your performance is a major mistake. Not only will it not help, but it's also very dangerous.

Sleep

Another performance cue that pilots can borrow from the athletes' playbook is the emphasis they put on getting adequate sleep. Athletes have long realized that, in addition to physical conditioning and sensible eating, the quality and amount of sleep they get plays a major role in their performance and results. The quality and amount of sleep athletes get can often be the key to winning.

While modern science cannot fully explain why we sleep, it generally accepts that it serves as a recovery period after being awake and prepares us for our next period of wakefulness. As such, our recent sleep history has a significant impact on our ability to perform at our peak.

Researchers have found that being awake for more than 16 hours significantly impacts our motor skills. Drivers who have been awake for 17–19 hours performed worse than those with a blood alcohol content of 0.05 percent. After 21 hours awake, our performance deteriorates to the level of having a blood alcohol content of 0.08 percent; 24 hours awake is equivalent to 0.10 percent!

It's not just staying awake for lengthy periods that results in this diminished capacity. Inadequate sleep for several days in a row can have the same negative effects. Once a sleep deficit develops, it is more difficult for the brain to function. Laboratory studies show that a single night of six hours sleep impacts a regular eight-hour-a-night sleeper's performance to the equivalent of having a 0.05 percent blood alcohol content. Average four hours of sleep a night for four or five days and your cognitive impairment is equivalent to having been awake for 24 hours. Ten days of accumulated sleep deprivation is equivalent to 48 hours without sleep.

Common causes of sleep deprivation among pilots include:
- Shift work (no need to remind airline pilots of this one!)
- Travel across time zones
- Personal choice ("burning the candle at both ends")
- Illnesses
- Sleep disorders
- Medications
- Sleeping environment (noise/temperature)
- Poor sleep hygiene (i.e., bad sleep habits)
- Disrupted sleep (e.g., baby in the home)
- Excessive thinking/worrying/planning (e.g., pre-test or pre-competition nerves)
- Unusual surroundings

Sleep deprivation presents itself in many ways, none of which are conducive to a peak piloting performance! Some of the symptoms particularly incompatible with flying include:
- Slowed reaction time
- Reduced speed and capacity for decision-making or problem-solving
- Poor concentration, inattentiveness, and reduced alertness
- Memory recall and retention problems (both short and long-term)
- Errors of omission due to forgetfulness
- Errors of commission due to impaired judgment
- Reduced situational awareness and spatial orientation
- Increased likelihood of mentally fixating on one thought
- Decrements in psychomotor skills

- Adverse physiological effects (vision problems, head and body aches, hallucinations, hand tremors)
- Adverse mood states (stress, depression, tension, confusion, fatigue, and anger)
- Sleep inertia and micro-sleeps

Most adults need an average of eight hours of restful sleep per night, although there is some individual variance (e.g., we tend to need less sleep as we get older). You should, however, use your state of alertness as your guide. If you sleep less than eight hours a night, fall asleep instantly, need an alarm clock to wake up, or are experiencing symptoms of sleep deprivation during your waking hours, then you can consider yourself sleep-deprived!

One way of determining the right amount of sleep for you is to spend a week waking up naturally without an alarm clock and keeping a sleep diary. Keeping a sleep diary involves recording the start and end time for all sleep periods (i.e., both night-time sleep and daytime naps). If you want to get accurate data on your hours of sleep, an electronic fitness/activity tracker can help. Worn as a bracelet, many of these trackers record data on both the quantity and restfulness of sleep. Over a week, if you average out the amount of sleep you get each night, you can determine a good start point for how much sleep your body needs per night.

Sleep scientists have established some strategies that pilots can effectively implement to ensure adequate rest for peak flying performance:

- **Establish a wake-up time:** Subconscious habits and body rhythms are strong determinants as to when you will fall asleep at night. The only thing we can consciously control is the time we get up. If your body has established an erratic sleeping pattern through insomnia, bad sleep habits, or irregular shift work, set an alarm for 30 minutes before your usual waking time. When it goes off, get up regardless of how much sleep you have had. Your body will eventually be forced to re-establish a normal sleeping pattern. Clinical research indicates this is the single-most effective strategy for curing insomnia.
- **Either optimize or avoid naps:** A quick nap can be a great way of boosting energy levels, improving alertness, reducing sleepiness, and improving cognitive performance. The optimum duration of a nap is 30 minutes. Taking longer naps is a sure fire way to disrupt your sleep pattern. Just like grazing through the day will spoil your appetite at meal time, napping will disrupt your natural sleep cycle at bedtime. If you are taking a nap in preparation for a night shift, then this is

not a consideration, but the timing of your nap will be. It is easiest to nap between two and five in the afternoon. Between seven and twelve o'clock in the morning and six and eight o'clock in the evening, your body resists attempts to nap.

- **Time your exercise:** Try and exercise every day as regular physical activity can promote more regular sleep and wake patterns (as well as reducing stress) but avoid exercise or vigorous activity three to four hours before bed as this awakens the body and makes it more difficult to fall asleep.

- **Caffeine, nicotine, alcohol and other drugs:** Caffeine (e.g., tea, coffee, chocolate, sodas, headache medicine) and nicotine are sleep disrupting stimulants and are best avoided four to five hours before sleep. Alcohol and sleep medications can initially induce sleep, but the ensuing sleep tends to be disrupted, fragmented, and unrefreshing. Alcohol should, therefore, be avoided at least four to six hours before bed and sleep medications avoided altogether.

- **Eat to sleep:** A by-product of the digestion of carbohydrates is the production of serotonin and serotonin makes us sleepy. The digestion of proteins has the opposite effect, inducing the production of less serotonin. A protein meal during the day may improve alertness and prevent you from dropping off in the afternoon, while a carbohydrate-heavy meal before bedtime should help you sleep. Eating large meals immediately before bedtime may also lead to insomnia.

- **Create the right environment for sleep:** We need the hormone melatonin to sleep, and we only release melatonin under low-light conditions. It is, therefore, important (imperative for shift workers trying to sleep during the day) that either our bedrooms are darkened using blackout curtains or that we wear an eye mask. Research has also found that we sleep best if we are warm in bed but the bedroom is cool. As you fall asleep, your body temperature drops. If your room is too hot, you can't lose body heat, and you won't sleep well. We should, therefore, utilize layers of bedding rather than adjust the room heater to achieve a comfortable temperature for sleep. You also need to choose pillows, mattresses, and bedding that are most comfortable for you. Many hotels now have pillow, mattress and bedding options to help guests in this matter.

- **Minimize sleep disruptions:** For pilots "living" in places like hotels or motels, large numbers of people coming and going add another element of difficulty to controlling your sleep environment. Block out unwanted sounds from within your room and beyond by utilizing a white-noise machine, earplugs, or even a small fan. Ask the switchboard to disable calls to your room and don't forget the "Do Not Disturb" sign on the door.

- **Establish a routine:** If you establish habits that you repeat in preparation for sleep every night, you will create strong body/mind associations between those habits and sleep. Examples could be visual cues such as laying out your pajamas on the bed or switching from main lights to bedside lamps. Other healthy sleep routines to establish would be going to bed and waking up as close as possible to the same time every day and only sleeping an hour longer than your regular waking time on days off. Obviously, a working pilot's schedule will have exceptions, but you should still strive for as much routine as possible to establish good sleep habits.

- **Bath before bedtime:** Sleep onset normally coincides with our body's natural temperature fall at night. A warm bath or shower about an hour before bedtime raises our body temperature slightly and steepens the natural temperature drop thus facilitating sleep.

- **Avoid stimulation before sleep:** While activities like phoning home, watching television, catching up on emails or surfing the net may seem relaxing to you, in reality, they provide stimulation and engage your mind. By avoiding stimulating activities 30 minutes before sleep, you will ensure that you don't begin to associate the bed with these activating tasks. Instead, do only mundane, unstimulating tasks or chores to allow your mind to slow down in preparation for sleep.

- **Relaxation:** There are numerous routines you can go through to remove some of the major roadblocks to sleep. Instead of lying awake dwelling on thoughts and worries you need to address, or chores you haven't done, put aside time before sleeping to write down anything on your mind so you can put it aside and address it the next day. Stretching, self-massage, or foam-rolling, muscle relaxation, and stress management techniques can relieve tension and help you fall asleep more quickly. Create the expectation of sound sleep by telling yourself that you are going to fall asleep easily and then wake before your alarm feeling alert and refreshed. If you wake up once or twice during the night, this is normal; don't get stressed about it.

- **Create associations between your bed and sleep:** As we have already stated, it is our subconscious habits and body rhythms that are the strongest determinant of when we fall asleep. Use your bed only for sleep or making love. Study in your office and watch television in your lounge room. If you're in a hotel, go to a café, hotel lobby, or sit at the desk in your room but leave the bed for sleep. Furthermore, if you aren't sleepy, don't go to bed. Once you do go to bed, if you can't sleep after 20 to 30 minutes, get back up. We can't force ourselves to sleep, so lying awake in bed only serves to create associations between your bed and sleeplessness. When establishing these habits, you may stay up later for a few days, but then natural sleepiness will start to occur earlier.

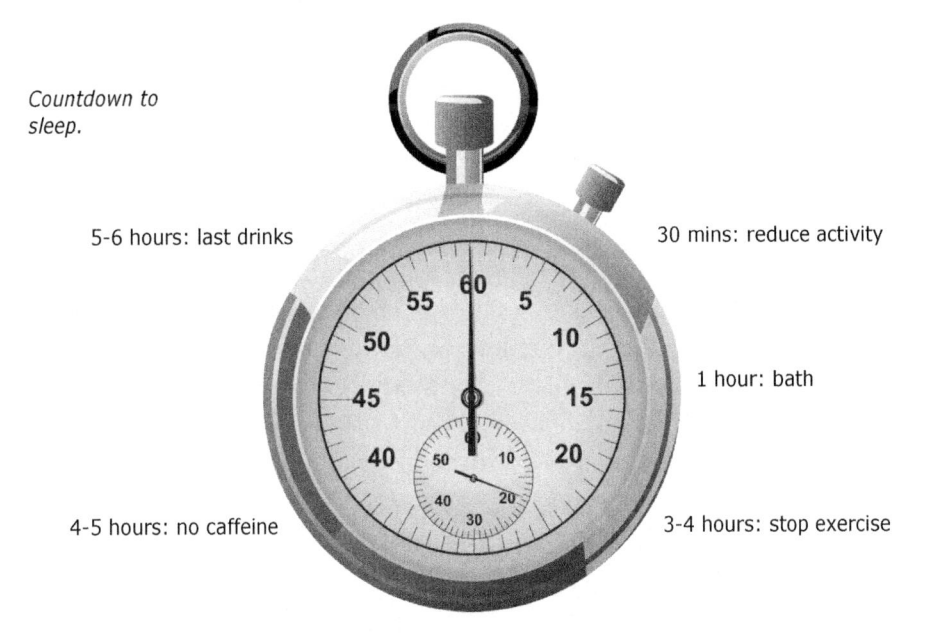

Countdown to sleep.

5-6 hours: last drinks

30 mins: reduce activity

1 hour: bath

4-5 hours: no caffeine

3-4 hours: stop exercise

We will close out our discussion on sleep with a relatively recent theory on overcoming jet lag. Scientists have based this theory on the internal food clock which helps animals regulate sleep. This food clock is largely dormant in humans but can be activated by controlled fasting. Scientists theorize that fasting on long-haul flights before eating at the next meal time of the new time zone can help quickly reset your internal clock. Food for thought?

Cockpit Comfort

Cockpit comfort may seem like a strange topic to cover in a book about peak performance flying but being comfortable in the aircraft is critical. If you're uncomfortable, not only will it take more physical energy to fly, it will also be overly tiring and affect you mentally. A painful body will reduce your concentration level. So, if you want to fly an aircraft to the best of your ability, you must first be seated properly in the cockpit or flight deck.

Aviation and motorsport have a lot in common and not just through shared engineering concepts, aerodynamics, and a closely-related history. Just like aviators, race drivers sit in the cockpits of expensive, sophisticated machinery while manipulating controls with their hands and feet. Just like aviators, feedback of a driver's control inputs comes from sensory perception and gauges. In Europe, both are called pilots, and you could never argue that race drivers are not operating at the extreme limits of performance! So, what can we learn about the importance of a good seat from these ground-bound pilots? Top pilots in Indy Car and Formula One will spend dozens of hours working to make their seat fit just right and then fine-tune it all season long.

Never underestimate the importance of your position and comfort in the aircraft seat, particularly when beginning a new type rating or endorsement. Many student pilots, or experienced pilots doing a new type rating, are so wrapped up in getting prepared for their first few lessons that they forget to pay attention to establishing a good seating position.

You receive much of the feedback from the aircraft through the seat. When you are sitting properly in a well-positioned seat, you will be more sensitive to the various vibrations and g-forces you need to interpret to ascertain what the aircraft is doing. Think about it. Your body has only three main contact points with the aircraft: the seat, the control yoke (or stick) and the rudder pedals.

Especially if you are flying air combat or aerobatics, you should use a seating position that puts as much of your body in contact with the aircraft as possible. You want to sit *in* the seat, not *on* it, with as much lateral support as possible, the limiting factor being the ability to move your arms freely.

Your shoulders should be back (not hunched forward) and your chin up. This position is the most efficient posture for flying an aircraft. It's where you are the strongest and most sensitive to the aircraft. A more laid back position is desirable for g-tolerance considerations when flying aerobatics. Reducing the vertical distance between the head and heart considerably improves g-tolerance. The ejector seat on the F-16 Fighting Falcon is reclined at 30 degrees for this very reason.

Your seating position should allow you to move the controls fully and freely without any interference, having to pull your shoulders off the seatback, or stretching to the limits of your reach. Check this with the seat belt or safety harness done up as tightly as you would use them when strapped in most securely.

You should also be able to fully depress the rudder pedals and actuate the brakes while still having a slight bend in your legs. This leg position is not only the least tiring (especially in an engine-out case for a multi-engine aircraft) but allows for ideal modulation of the brakes as you will be able to depress them by pivoting your feet at the ankles, not moving your entire leg in mid-air. You want to use the balls of your feet on the pedals. They are the strongest and most sensitive part of the foot.

If you are a competition aerobatics pilot or air racer, it is worth investigating the possibility of having a seat or seat insert custom-built for you. With a little thought and preparation, you can mold a seat yourself using expandable foam. This simple operation can greatly improve your flying performance. Use a two-part foam (available at fiberglass shops) poured into a plastic bag between your body and the seat shell or cockpit tub to form a solid polyurethane shell. Before pouring, be sure to cover everything (and we mean everything!) with plastic garbage bags as the foam is practically impossible to remove after it has set onto something. Upon removing the plastic bags, you can trim off the excess and use the body-shaped foam as either a seat insert or as a mold to make a carbon-fiber or fiberglass seat (if allowed by the aviation regulators in the country in which you live). Special memory-foam cushions made especially for pilots are also worth considering. One advantage of these is that you can carry them with you and use them in multiple aircraft types you might fly. You may want to ascertain the fire resistance of the material of manufacture.

Anytime you modify or adjust your seating position on the ground, you have to realize it will only be on the runway and in the air that you will know for sure how it feels. Once you have a seating position that works for you, make sure you jot down some notes on how to recreate this seating position consistently. Are there certain parts of the aircraft cockpit that line up when in this position? What can you see in your peripheral vision that would help you recreate this position? Where are you looking in relation to the glare shield? How many clicks up or forward is the seat if it has set positions? How many winds from full forward or aft is the rudder pedal adjustment? Manufacturers of more sophisticated aircraft may have fitted eye guides for lining up an ideal eye position. If your aircraft has them, use them.

Tarmacs are dirty and greasy areas so make sure you check your feet before climbing into your seat. Make sure that both the pedals and the bottom of your shoes are dry and clean. Having wet or greasy feet slipping on the rudder pedals or brakes does not lend itself to a peak performance on the runway or in the air! Aerobatic, air race, or fighter pilots may even want to resort to having a crewmember wipe their shoes with a clean rag before getting into the aircraft. Once again using a motorsport example, at wet races, Formula One drivers are sometimes seen being taken to their cars on a cart and being lifted straight from the cart into the cockpit of the car so that their feet won't get wet. Others wear plastic bags over their shoes.

PERFORMANCE TIP

Establish a good seating position.

Not only are the safety harnesses in an aircraft there in case of a crash, but they also help support your body. If you own your aircraft, only use the very best seat belts and take good care of them. Keep them clean and inspect them often for wear and damage. Adjust them so they hold your body firmly and comfortably. Remember, they will stretch and loosen throughout the progression of a flight (particularly the shoulder harnesses) so ensure you can reach down and tighten them while flying.

If the type of flying you do involves abrupt or violent maneuvering, make sure any part of the cockpit that you could come in contact with during a flight is covered with a high-density foam rubber or consider wearing knee or elbow pads. Bruising and pain are not conducive to good concentration over a long weekend of flying competition aerobatics!

What you wear when you fly is also a consideration for cockpit comfort. Make sure that what you wear won't restrict your body movements while moving the controls through their full range of motion. Also, check that you don't have belts, buttons, or zips positioned where they will create pressure points under your harness. A one-piece flight suit can increase comfort for aerobatics in addition to ensuring that you use zipped pockets to safely stow any objects that would otherwise come loose while maneuvering.

A good set of sunglasses or tinted helmet visor is a must for flying in glare conditions. A lightweight helmet is something you should consider if doing aerobatics as you don't need the distraction of headsets and sunglasses moving or coming free in the middle of a maneuver.

Other possible sources of sensory stimuli which will reduce performance, and therefore should be considerations for cockpit comfort, are excessive noise, vibration, and odors. Is your hearing protection adequate? What can you do to help eliminate vibration and smells entering the cockpit?

If you wear a parachute when you fly, as many competition aerobatic pilots do, make use of a qualified rigger to ensure it is both comfortable and worn correctly. Not all parachutes are equal; some are quite comfortable, and some are like sitting on a bag of potatoes (which would quite obviously be an unwelcome distraction when trying to concentrate fully on the task at hand). The parachute may even form part of the seat, and there are companies that can make custom cushioning to go with the parachute/seat combination.

Finally, do everything possible to help keep the cockpit temperature comfortable. If it is hot, make sure the air ducts are functioning and positioned to direct air at you. A hot or cold cockpit of an aircraft will adversely affect your stamina and performance.

The Peak Performance Pilot

Imagine the pilot operating at the absolute peak of their profession. What makes them different from the average pilot? Let's assume we are all born with the same amount of natural flying talent. Assuming we have the basic physical design, we all have the ability to be a flying superstar, a peak performance pilot. In other words, no one is born to be a pilot. If there is a difference between our peak performance pilot and you today, it is simply a result of what the two of you have done with the talent with which you were born. There were probably several events in the peak performance pilot's life that have enabled them to take the basic talent they were born with and turn that talent into the superstar piloting abilities they demonstrate today.

You now know the value of being integrated (whole-brained) to achieving peak performance. Many children do not do enough integrating physical movement as babies to become as integrated as possible. The baby that does not do much "cross-crawling" action may not become as integrated as early in life. This lack of integration leads to a child who might stay away from physical activities because they have formed a belief that, "I'm not very good at it."

Our peak performance pilot develops along a very different path. As a small child, they become integrated. The child feels and acts more coordinated. Comments from outside sources (parents, friends, coaches, etc.) serve to reinforce this belief system. They are encouraged to participate in numerous sports which leads to the further development of their coordination and sensory input skills. Success encourages the child to do even more physical movement which even further enhances brain integration.

When our peak performance pilot began flying lessons, one of the things that separated them from their peers was their ability to learn so very quickly - more quickly than most everyone else. Learning to fly, they used well-defined, strategic, deliberate practice time. They used specific strategies for improving.

We're not suggesting that our peak performance pilot necessarily developed these abilities at a conscious level. We guess they "stumbled" into most of the techniques, just like many people do who become good at a physical task. On top of that, we suspect they learned some techniques in a very specific manner.

You see, much of the development of the peak performance pilot's natural talent was a result of the environment they grew up in and the learning strategies they used. Assuming they started life with the same talent level as everyone around them, they were able to take that talent and develop it and enhance it faster.

The main ingredient that superstars of any pursuit have (that mere stars may not) is the ability to learn quickly. That is what gives them the edge. It doesn't matter how much natural talent you believe you were born with, it is what you do with that talent that will determine the result. If you learn how to learn, and learn how to be better and smarter than other people with similar talent, you will be miles ahead.

Of course, the ability to learn quickly is not enough on its own. Peak performance in any pursuit doesn't happen without some effort. Our peak performance pilot is probably well-known for the amount of time they spend working out physically and preparing mentally. You can probably think of a pilot you know, admire, or even envy that fits the description of our peak performance pilot. When you look at all the hard work they have

PERFORMANCE TIP
Learn how to learn, and you will never stop improving.

> **PERFORMANCE TIP**
>
> Be open to ever-improvement.

put into developing their ability you have to ask, "Is that natural talent or hard work that got them to where they are?"

Have you ever seen a young and upcoming sportsperson who seems destined for greatness but whose career fizzles out to nothing? Their early performances appear to be effortless and gifted, and yet they just don't cut it in the big league when destiny calls. This outcome tends to support the theory that it's not how much talent you're born with that's going to make the difference, it's what you do with that talent.

To do anything with your talent, you need to begin with an open or growth-oriented mindset - a mindset that is constantly looking for ways to improve. It's a mindset of wanting to work harder at becoming better than anyone else. It's an understanding that it's through effort that any amount of talent you currently have will turn into something special. It's knowing that, no matter how easy it's been to be successful so far, you now need to work harder than anyone else to get to the very top. That's the attitude that every great champion or superstar has ever had.

The aviation world is littered with pilots who were successful early in their careers, developed an attitude of, "I'm great, I'm gifted, and therefore I will make it to the top with this natural talent," but didn't amount to anything or even left the profession altogether. It takes commitment to doing what it takes to become as successful as you desire. It's going to take effort; it's going to take an open mind, even a craving, for learning and improvement. A desire to learn is a critical factor to success. It can inspire you to do whatever it takes to prepare.

There's also no doubt that your level of success is directly proportional to your level of preparation. It's no fluke that interviews with successful athletes will often focus on their preparation. Success and preparation come together. That's all well and good for professional athletes who spend all their waking hours preparing to win, you say, but what about the poor amateur pilot?

The pilot operating at their peak never quits trying to get better still. If you want to be the world aerobatic champion or win the Reno Air Races, that's a given. What isn't a given is the attitude that even the most low-key amateur pilot needs to perform at their peak or just to have more fun. If thirty minutes a day is too much for you to commit to being the best pilot you possibly can be then, that's okay. As long as you realize that you won't improve much without some commitment of time to prepare. It's okay as long as you don't feel bitter or frustrated that you're not improving as much or as quickly as other pilots who probably *are* committing time for preparation. We can't emphasize this enough: the more you put into becoming a better pilot, the more fun you will have.

One of the things that will help you succeed in reaching your peak as a pilot is not letting your current successes or setbacks affect your attitude or mindset. You need to see the positives in practically everything that happens to you. If you're not performing as you would like, happily focus on making things better. If you are performing well, happily focus on performing even better still. Your concentration of effort should always be on thinking about how you can always be performing better. The key is that you need to be always improving. Remember also to concentrate on performance over results. Great pilots focus more energy on ensuring their performance is at its maximum, trusting that that will look after the results, rather than any other focus. They know that they can't control the results, but they can control their performance and ultimately it is their performance that will dictate the result.

> **PERFORMANCE TIP**
> *The more you put into becoming a better pilot, the more fun you will have!*

You can also be sure that successful athletes included mental imagery as part of their preparation. You can use mental imagery to change your focus away from the results and onto your performance. Rather than doing mental imagery of achieving a certain result, do mental imagery of flying the aircraft perfectly. So, rather than having expectations, you are focused on your potential, on the possibilities. Rather than focusing on the result, see, feel, and hear yourself performing at your best, no matter what the conditions or competition levels are. Be open to whatever could happen if you perform at your very best, flying the aircraft consistently and accurately.

You also need to take full responsibility for whatever happens, good or bad, and not make excuses. What matters is performing at one's best, learning how to become even better, and not blaming others for what happens.

Before you close your mind to what we've just said and think, "Oh, that's fine for a young pilot who's trying to become the next big thing, I just want to have fun doing what I do at my level," think again. There are just as many amateur pilots who are putting in the effort to improve as there are young, up-and-coming world aerobatic champions. All around the world, there are amateur pilots, pilots who are older, pilots who are not out to become world aerobatic champions who still have the attitude that they can improve and are willing to do what it takes to do so. Why? For one reason, it's more fun! In the end, that's why anyone should fly and why you should put in the effort it takes to be successful: to have fun.

> **PERFORMANCE TIP**
> *Have Fun!*

Appendix A: Performance Tips

- The better the quality and the more quantity of input from your senses that you can process, the better the output and the better your performance will be. [p15]
- Every day, practice being aware. [p30]
- The more reference points you have, the fewer errors you will make. [p37]
- Minimize errors through maximizing sensory input. [p37]
- The better the information your senses provide to your brain, the more sensitive you'll be to what the aircraft is doing and what it needs. [p38]
- Use g-sensing sessions to improve your ability to fly at the appropriate g-load for the maneuver you're flying. [p44]
- Practice doesn't make perfect; only perfect practice makes perfect. [p51]
- Fly in your mind before flying in the aircraft. [p54]
- The more you learn, the better you get; the better you get, the more successful you will be. Focus on learning and success will follow. [p73]
- MI + A = G [p80]
- If it seems you're not improving, you're about to. [p83]
- If a change doesn't work the first time, rethink and retry. [p85]
- Sensory input and awareness are the keys to flying proficiently, no matter what the maneuver is. [p88]
- The better your programming, the better you'll perform in pressure situations. [p89]
- Natural talent is just more (and better) practice. [p90]
- What you practice is just as important as how much you practice. [p91]
- Increase your awareness by debriefing. [p95]
- Preparation is not just one thing; it's everything. [p99]
- Practice how you plan to test and then you'll test as you practiced. [p100]
- Replay past successes to trigger a performance state of mind. [p103]
- Develop and use a Pre-Planned Thought (PPT). [p104]
- Make your thoughts non-judgmental. [p105]
- Replace negatively-phrased instructions and thoughts with positively-framed ones. Focus on what you want. [p106]
- Practice is programming. [p107]
- Relax, use less effort, and just let it happen. [p109]
- Challenge + Belief = Flow [p111]
- Focus on your performance and the results will look after themselves. [p114]
- Don't set expectations; focus on the possibilities and your potential. [p116]
- What you believe is what you get. [p121]
- Whether you believe you can or believe you can't, either way you're correct. [p122]
- Stretch your belief system, bit by bit, through self-talk and mental programming. [p124]
- Use your strengths to program over the top of weaknesses. [p125]
- If you need to optimize performance, explore the aircraft's behavior. [p130]
- Be comfortable being uncomfortable. [p130]
- Be prepared by preparing mentally. [p131]
- Focus on what you love about flying. [p134]

Appendix A: Performance Tips

- If you want to perform at your absolute peak, you owe it to yourself to be as physically fit as possible. [p140]
- Establish a good seating position. [p148]
- Learn how to learn, and you will never stop improving. [p151]
- Be open to ever-improvement. [p152]
- The more you put into becoming a better pilot, the more fun you will have! [p153]
- Have fun! [p153]

Appendix B: Self-Coaching

This list of sample self-coaching questions is not meant to be definitive or exhaustive. It serves purely to act as a guide to get you started developing your own list of self-coaching questions best suited to your needs.

Pre-Flight and Engine Start
- Did I ensure that all required documentation was on board?
- Did I obtain pertinent weather forecasts and correctly interpret them?
- Was my flight planning accurate and complete?
- Was my fuel order legal and sufficient?
- Was the loaded fuel loaded verified against fuel order?
- Was airworthiness checked and correct dispatch deviation procedures applied?
- Were all items of the pre-flight inspection performed correctly?
- Were my performance calculations correct?
- Were weight and balance calculations correctly performed?
- Did I brief all appropriate and pertinent information?
- Were radio aids correctly set and identified for departure?
- Was the flight management system correctly loaded and utilized?
- Was the engine start procedure applied correctly?
- Did I plan for and (self-) brief contingency procedures?

Taxiing for Departure
- Can I ease on/off the brake pedal more gently?
- How is my directional control?
- How is my speed control?
- Am I using throttle against brakes?
- Did I apply appropriate safety procedures crossing runways (e.g., lookout and strobes on)?

Take-Off and Climb
- Did I cross check runway in use and clearances?
- Were hot or cold weather procedures applied (where applicable)?
- Did I assess the visibility requirements were met?
- Did I check the windsock against aircraft crosswind limits and wind used for performance calculations?

Appendix B: Self-Coaching

Take-Off and Climb continued
- Did I correctly apply take-off minima?
- Did I line up on the centerline?
- Do I smoothly apply power?
- Do I sufficiently allow for torque affect?
- How far ahead do I look when taking off?
- Can I look farther ahead?
- Is my crosswind technique appropriate?
- Were correct multi-crew callouts made?
- Is my rotation rate appropriate?
- Did I attain and maintain the desired target attitude?
- Was my transition from visual to instrument flight smoothly flown?
- If applicable, were correct contingency procedures applied (e.g., RTO or EFATO)?
- How is my speed maintenance in the climb?
- Was the power reduction and gear/flap, retraction sequence correctly applied?
- Did I meet all the necessary altimetry requirements?
- Were appropriate autoflight modes used on departure?
- Did I comply with all applicable noise abatement, SID, and ATC departure requirements?
- How is my level off from the climb?
- Were correct procedures applied at transition altitude and top-of-climb?

Cruise
- Did I monitor the flight progress (navigation, fuel and communications logs)?
- Did I comply with all ATC instructions?
- Did I obtain updated and relevant weather forecasts?
- Did I satisfy LSALT requirements?
- How was my track keeping?
- How was my altitude maintenance?
- How was my speed control?
- Did I apply the correct turbulence penetration and weather avoidance techniques?
- Did I comply with all state requirements?
- Did I make appropriate use of the flight management system?
- Was the aircraft operated within its limitations envelope?
- Did I comply with relevant rules of the air (e.g., right-of-way, ETOPS, RNP, RVSM)?
- Did I remember to notify my company of arrival requirements?

Maneuvers
- Is my lookout adequate?
- How consistent is my maneuver entry speed?
- What is my rate of g-application?
- What would happen if I changed my entry parameters? Speed? G-load?
- Should my control inputs be smoother or crisper?
- Exactly where should my reference points be?

Appendix B: Self-Coaching

Maneuvers continued
- Where should I be looking at each stage? Am I?
- Did I exit my figures on line?
- What can I do to perfect the entry, mid, and exit phases?
- Did I respect my minimum operational height?

Descent and Arrival
- Was weather for destination and alternate airports obtained?
- Were the correct charts selected for STAR and arrival?
- Was the flight management system correctly loaded for arrival?
- Was the required landing distance correctly evaluated?
- Was my calculated top-of-descent sufficiently accurate?
- Did I make all applicable altimetry calls at intermediate levels?
- Was the correct transition level procedure applied?
- Did I adhere to all company and state speed limits?
- Were navigation aids correctly tuned and identified?
- Did I perform all required procedures/checklists?

Instrument Approaches
- Was my brief relevant and contain all pertinent information?
- Did I fly the correct sector entry?
- Did I comply with all holding pattern and approach tolerances?
- What altitude tolerance did I maintain on approach?
- What tracking tolerance did I maintain on approach?
- Was my glideslope retention satisfactory?
- Did I make all applicable multi-crew low visibility and instrument procedure calls?
- Did I monitor the navigation aids or RAIM as required?
- Did I correctly apply landing minima?

Traffic Patterns and Circling Approaches
- Was my traffic pattern entry procedure correct?
- How much angle of bank am I using on crosswind and base? Is it adequate?
- How is my downwind spacing?
- How is my altitude maintenance and tracking?
- Is my traffic awareness adequate?
- Where am I turning base?
- Should I be turning base earlier or later?
- How is my speed control around base?
- Do I roll out on centerline?
- How is my go-around procedure?

Landing
- Did I confirm correct landing runway?
- How is my speed and aim-point maintenance on final?

Appendix B: Self-Coaching

Landing continued
- Did I fly a stable approach?
- Is my crosswind technique appropriate?
- What height did I cross the threshold?
- Did I cross the threshold on the centerline?
- Are my flare height and rate appropriate?
- How far ahead do I look in the flare and on rollout when landing?
- Can I look farther ahead?
- Do I select the thrust levers to idle at an appropriate time?
- Where am I touching down?
- Was the touchdown soft, smooth, positive, firm, or hard?
- Do I touchdown on the centerline?
- Is my stopping technique adequate?
- Did I use equal braking pressure with both brakes?
- Were all applicable multi-crew call outs made on the rollout?

Taxi-in and Post Flight
- Can I ease on/off the brake pedal more gently?
- How is my directional control?
- How is my speed control?
- Am I using throttle against brakes?
- Did I apply appropriate safety procedures crossing runways (e.g., lookout and strobes on)?
- Did I correctly complete all procedural items for this phase-of-flight?
- How accurately did I park?
- Did I perform all required procedures/checklists?
- Did I correctly complete all post flight paperwork?
- Did I establish realistic learning objectives for the flight?
- Was my fuel planning adequate?
- Was the flight accomplished within duty time limits?

General or Multi-Phase Applicable
- When was the last time I worked on developing (practicing) my sensory awareness?
- Where am I in the continuous learning process loop?
- How tightly do I grip the controls in each phase of flight?
- Can I relax my grip a bit?
- Can I manipulate the controls more smoothly?
- Am I coordinating my turns and keeping the aircraft balanced?
- On speed and power changes, do I apply appropriate rudder inputs?
- How is my checklist management?
- What memory cues can I use to ensure I don't miss any procedural steps?
- Did I maintain situational awareness?
- Did I respect airframe and engine limitations?
- Was my lookout and traffic awareness adequate?

Appendix B: Self-Coaching

General or Multi-Phase Applicable continued
- Did I comply with VFR/IFR rules?
- Did I use correct phraseology in my radiotelephony?
- Did I correctly use the weather radar?
- Did I communicate effectively with other crew members throughout the flight?
- Did I use appropriate levels of automation for each phase of flight?
- Did I acknowledge and verify flight mode annunciations?
- Did I maintain flight mode awareness throughout the flight?
- Did I remember to use anti-ice and de-ice as appropriate?
- Were any non-normal conditions, systems anomalies or parameter exceedances picked up and the correct handling procedures applied?
- Did I apply appropriate task prioritization?

Appendix C: Resources

Internet
www.performancepilot.net

Books
Brain Gym, Teacher's Edition, Paul E. Dennison and Gail E. Dennison
Flow In Sports, Susan A. Jackson and Mihaly Csikszentmihalyi
Flow, Mihaly Csikszentmihalyi
Inner Tennis, Timothy Gallwey
Lessons From The Art Of Juggling, Michael J. Gelb and Tony Buzan
Mindset, Carol Dweck
Motorsports Medicine, Dr. Harlen Hunter & Rick Stoff
Outliers: The Story of Success, Malcolm Gladwell
Peak: Secrets from the New Science of Expertise, Anders Ericsson
Smart Moves, Carla Hannaford
Talent Is Overrated, Geoff Colvin
The Dominance Factor, Carla Hannaford
The High Performance Mind, Anna Wise
The Open Mind, Dawna Markova
The Power Behind Your Eyes, Robert-Michael Kaplan
Thinking Body, Dancing Mind, Chungliang Al Huang and Jerry Lynch

Acknowledgements

A huge thank you to Andrew, Anthony, Barry, Brent, Chris, Feng, George, Jaimie, Mark, Marq, Maz, Robin, Russell, Thomas, and Zoë. Our book is all the better for your invaluable contributions.

Summary

PERFORMANCE PILOT
www.performancepilot.net

THREE KEYS TO IMPROVING PERFORMANCE

QUALITY INPUT

Visual

Lazy-8s
- Time: 20-30 seconds each hand; 20-30 second both hands
- When: Morning, evening & before a flight

Visual Exercises
Practice being aware; consciously stretch your vision
- Time: Everyday activities
- When: Every day

Sensory Input Sessions
Debrief & note everything you see
- Time: 10-15 minutes
- When: Regularly

FASTER PROCESSING

Cross Crawls
Start at a comfortable rate, slow down, and then speed up till almost running pace.
- Time: 30 seconds
- When: Morning, evening & before a flight

Head & Eye Integration
- Phase 1: Eyes left, head right
- Phase 2: Eyes right, head left
- Phase 3: Eyes up, head down
- Phase 4: Eyes down, head up

Random order and varying speeds
- Time: Before a flight

Centering
Center yourself by placing your tongue on the roof of your mouth.
- Time: As required to relieve stress or relax and regularly when you need to be integrated
- When: Times of high stress and workload

Auditory

Ear Plugs
Learn to construct information from restricted auditory input

Defect Retraining
Adjust TV volume over time with a goal of watching at conversational volume

Sensory Input Sessions
Debrief & note everything you see
- Time: 10-15 minutes
- When: Regularly

Kinesthetic

Wear Gloves
Wear thicker gloves to improve tactile handling

Light Touch
Lightest touch possible on controls to increase sensitivity & kinesthetic perception
- When: Habitually

Barefoot Walking
To improve sensory input, balance and proprioception
- Time: 20-30 minutes
- When: Several times a week

Sensory Input Sessions
Debrief & note everything you see
- Time: 10-15 minutes
- When: Regularly

G-SENSING

Juggling
- Time: 5 minutes
- When: Daily

Table Tennis
Ramp up speed of play
- When: Regularly

Simulator
Turn down volume & learn to construct information from non-auditory input

POWER + ATTITUDE SENSING

QUALITY PROGRAMMING

Mental Imagery
- Establish goals
- Write a narrative
- Memorize or record the script
- Determine triggers
  - Word
  - Action
  - Visual Cue
- Establish environment to build muscle memory
  - Props
  - Control column
  - Wall panels
- Alpha-theta state
- Allocate days for specific skill building or technique practice
- Time: Hour + between sessions
- When: Morning, evening, daily

Perfect Practice
Only perfect practice makes perfect

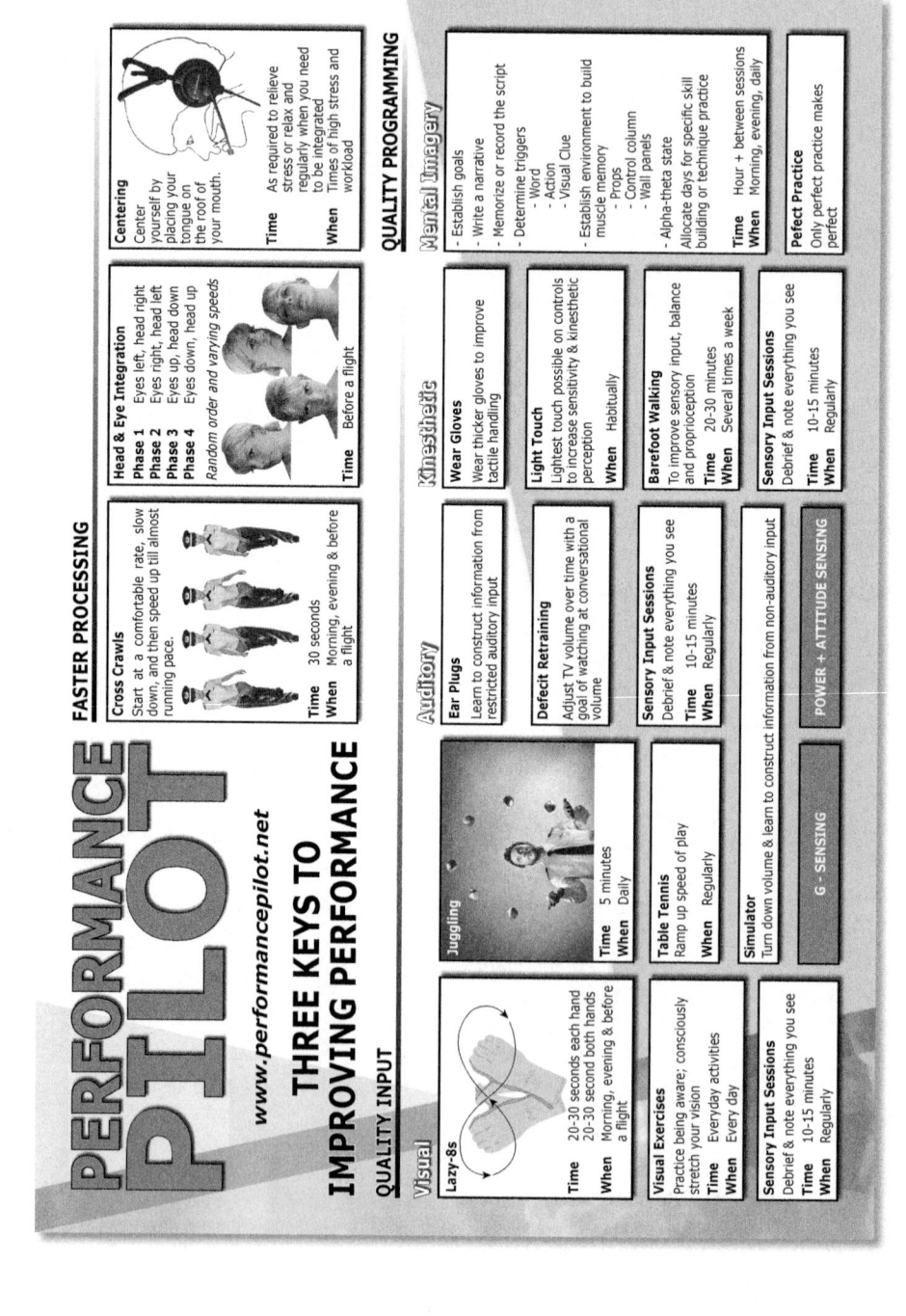

Download this summary from www.performancepilot.net/summary

Summary

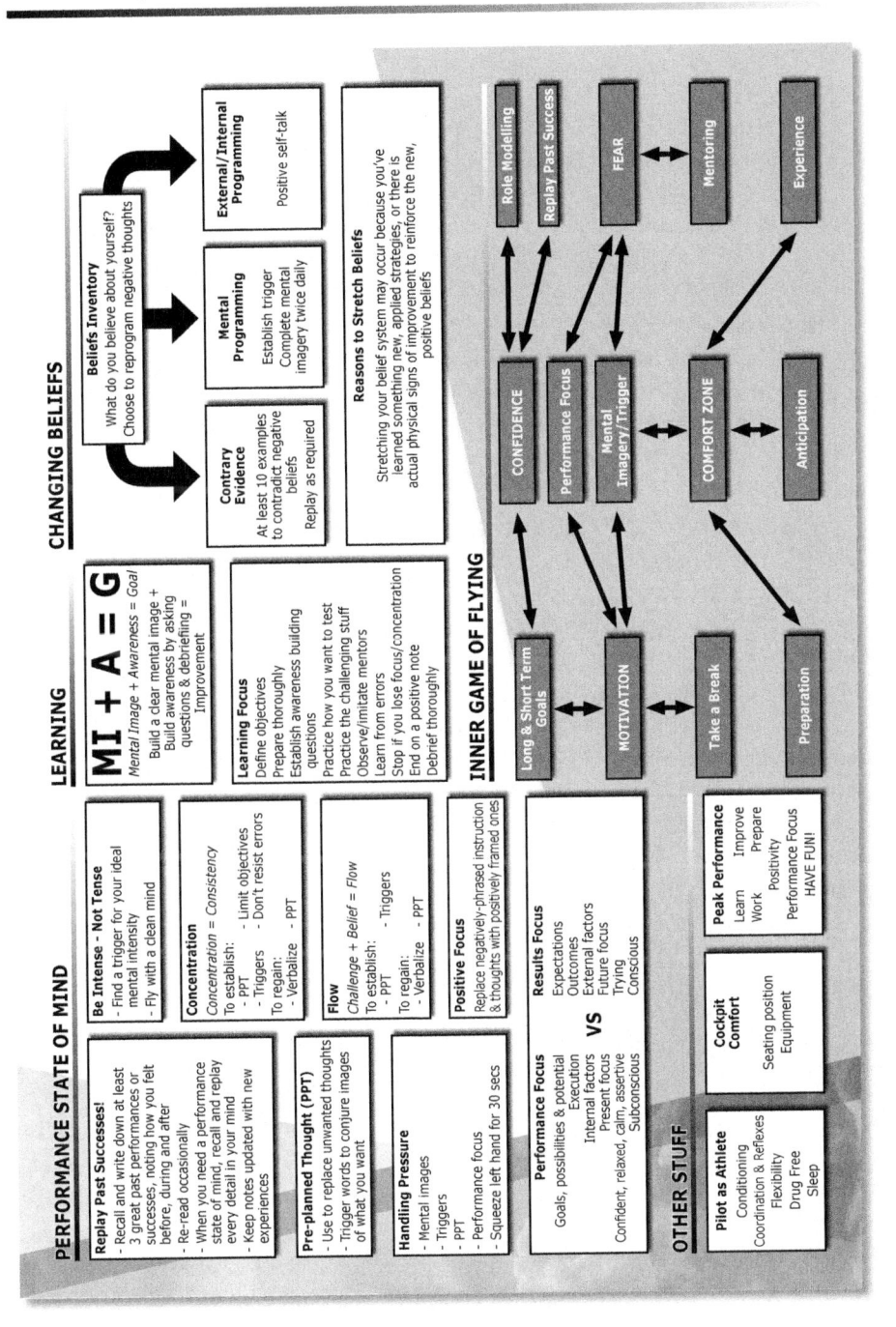

PERFORMANCE STATE OF MIND

Replay Past Successes!
- Recall and write down at least 3 great past performances or successes, noting how you felt before, during and after
- Re-read occasionally
- When you need a performance state of mind, recall and replay every detail in your mind
- Keep notes updated with new experiences

Be Intense - Not Tense
- Find a trigger for your ideal mental intensity
- Fly with a clean mind

Concentration
Concentration = Consistency
- To establish:
  - PPT
  - Triggers
- To regain:
  - Verbalize
- Limit objectives
- Don't resist errors
- PPT

Flow
Challenge + Belief = Flow
- To establish:
  - PPT
  - Triggers
- To regain:
  - Verbalize
  - PPT

Positive Focus
Replace negatively-phrased instruction & thoughts with positively framed ones

Pre-planned Thought (PPT)
- Use to replace unwanted thoughts
- Trigger words to conjure images of what you want

Handling Pressure
- Mental images
- Triggers
- PPT
- Performance focus
- Squeeze left hand for 30 secs

Performance Focus vs **Results Focus**

Performance Focus:
Goals, possibilities & potential
Execution
Internal factors
Present focus
Confident, relaxed, calm, assertive
Subconscious

Results Focus:
Expectations
Outcomes
External factors
Future focus
Trying
Conscious

Peak Performance
Learn Improve
Work Prepare
Positivity
Performance Focus
HAVE FUN!

LEARNING

$$MI + A = G$$
Mental Image + Awareness = Goal
Build a clear mental image + Build awareness by asking questions & debriefing = Improvement

Learning Focus
- Define objectives
- Prepare thoroughly
- Establish awareness building questions
- Practice how you want to test
- Practice the challenging stuff
- Observe/imitate mentors
- Learn from errors
- Stop if you lose focus/concentration
- End on a positive note
- Debrief thoroughly

CHANGING BELIEFS

Beliefs Inventory
What do you believe about yourself?
Choose to reprogram negative thoughts

Contrary Evidence
At least 10 examples to contradict negative beliefs
Replay as required

Mental Programming
Establish trigger
Complete mental imagery twice daily

External/Internal Programming
Positive self-talk

Reasons to Stretch Beliefs
Stretching your belief system may occur because you've learned something new, applied strategies, or there is actual physical signs of improvement to reinforce the new, positive beliefs

INNER GAME OF FLYING

Role Modelling ↔ Replay Past Success
↕
CONFIDENCE ↔ Performance Focus ↔ Mental Imagery/Trigger ↔ COMFORT ZONE ↔ Anticipation
↕
Long & Short Term Goals ↔ MOTIVATION ↔ Take a Break ↔ Preparation
↕
FEAR ↔ Mentoring ↔ Experience

OTHER STUFF

Pilot as Athlete
Conditioning
Coordination & Reflexes
Flexibility
Drug Free
Sleep

Cockpit Comfort
Seating position
Equipment

Download this summary from www.performancepilot.net/summary

About the Authors

Ross Bentley

In 30 years, Ross has had four parallel careers. The most visible has been as a professional race car driver. Ross pursued a dream that he'd had since he was five years old: to race Indy Cars. He reached that goal in the early 90s, racing against the likes of Mario and Michael Andretti, Al Unser Jr, Nigel Mansell, Emerson Fittipaldi and Bobby Rahal. He then moved to racing sports cars, winning the 1998 United States Road Racing Championship, driving for the factory-backed PTG BMW M3 team. A definite highlight was winning the Rolex 24 Hours at Daytona in 2003.

His least-visible career is as entrepreneur and business owner. Ross is the founder, or co-founder, and builder of five companies. Through all phases of a business, from initial concept to planning stages, and through funding to maturation, he's lived the adrenaline rush of the start-up, as well as the trials and tribulations of growth and day-to-day operations. While each company has had its challenges, it's what he's learned from the experiences that have been most meaningful to him.

Ross is also an established author. In 1997, he wrote his first book, *Speed Secrets*, about the art and science of race car driving. Since then, he's added seven more titles to the series, as well as one on karting. Ross loves to write and, at the time of publication, is currently working on a few more projects, including those focused on performance in the workplace for leaders, managers, and employees.

Finally, Ross is a performance coach. He could never have predicted where his coaching career would take him. Besides travelling all over North America, he's been to Australia, Korea, China and Europe to coach. Ross has coached amateur and professional race car drivers and motorcycle racers, young and old. He's even coached coaches. Ross's performance coaching is not just confined to motorsport. He has also coached athletes (from lacrosse to racquetball to tennis), CEOs, business owners, first-time managers, employees who were struggling, and pilots!

Ross enjoys sharing his knowledge and experience, whether he's conducting a seminar or giving a keynote speech. He has presented to corporate sales teams, government agencies, military flying units, service clubs, at industry conferences, and to a variety of automotive groups.

As a self-confessed learning junkie, Ross has extensively studied neuroscience, kinesiology, business practices, management technique, marketing, finance, sports psychology, coaching, and human learning. Ross's specialty, however, is in bringing out the best performance in individuals and teams, no matter the environment. His overriding passion is performance.

About the Authors

Phil Wilkes

Phil is a professional pilot. His eclectic flying career has spanned both military and civil aviation, in regional, domestic, and international operations. In the military, Phil was the academic dux of his pilot course and flew both jet-trainers and as the captain of military transport aircraft. The general-aviation phase of his career included low-level aerial power-line survey, managing and flying for a flying school and charter business, and fly-in fly-out staff changeovers for mining companies. He has flown turbo-props for a night freighter company and for a regional airline with the longest route structure of any turbo-props-based airline in the world. He has also flown both short and long haul types for the most iconic of Australian carriers.

Over his nearly 30 years as a pilot, to date, Phil has logged over 13,000 hours in 30 different types including HS748, Metro 23, Fokker Friendship, Shorts 360, DHC8, Boeing 747 (pilot and flight engineer licenses), Boeing 737 and Airbus A330. Phil also has considerable experience teaching aircraft systems and performance as well as aerodynamics. Phil loves to teach, holds a Certificate in Vocational Instruction, and has also worked as a management and leadership trainer in a military officer training establishment, driving coach, and ski instructor.

In his spare time, Phil is an amateur race car driver and used the techniques in Ross's motorsport books to achieve three state titles and a Rookie of the Year award. It was Phil's exposure to Ross's books that lead to their collaboration on this book for pilots.

Index

Ab initio, 91
Abnormal, 8, 16, 51, 52, 58, 59, 61, 64, 69, 80, 104, 124, 147, 159
Aches, 138, 139, 142
Activity tracker, 142
Actualization, 17, 99
Adverse aileron yaw, 23, 49
Adversity, 136
Aerial combat. *See* Combat
Aerobatics, 1, 8, 9, 29, 34, 41, 43–44, 52, 53, 54, 64, 66, 86, 91, 95, 98, 115, 121, 124, 125, 129, 130, 131, 133, 136, 137, 139, 147–49, 152–53
Aerobics. *See* Fitness
Aerodynamics, 146, 163
Aim point, 28, 39, 73, 77–80, 87–88, 105
Air combat. *See* Combat
Air force, 1, 51, 54, 68, 76
Air racing, 9, 52, 53, 61, 132, 139, 147–48, 152
Air traffic control, 8, 97
Airbus
  A320, 1, 34, 88, 87–88
  A330, 30, 40, 78, 163
  A380, 69
Airlines, 1, 9, 16, 21, 34, 54, 68, 76, 93, 133, 141, 163
Airmanship, 1
Airspeed. *See* Speed
Alcohol, 140, 143
Alertness, 31, 138, 141–44
Altimetry, 99, 156, 157
Altitude, 24, 38, 40, 51, 80, 87, 103, 128, 132, 156, 157
Andretti
  Mario, 162
  Michael, 162
Anger, 101, 142
Angle of bank. *See* Turning
Anticipation, 8, 125, 128, 139
Anxiety, 101, 108, 115, 117, 129
Approaches, 8, 24, 26, 27, 28, 30, 40, 59, 69–70, 78, 80, 93, 157, 158

Aptitude, 120
Armchair flying. *See* Mental imagery
Arms, 23, 43, 139, 147
Armstrong, Neil, 132
Arousal, 59, 116, 117
Art, 18
Assertiveness, 58, 114, 135
Athletes, 10, 19, 55, 57, 89, 98, 105, 109, 112–13, 115, 116, 119, 120, 137–45, 152–53, 162
Atmospheric conditions, 8, 30, 42–43, 50, 64, 69, 74, 80, 84, 97, 105, 115, 121, 125, 129, 130–31, 139, 153, 155–56, 156, 157, 158
Attention, 91, 105, 117, 141
Attitude
  Aircraft, 8, 36, 38, 40–43, 60, 88, 94, 156
  Personal, 58, 107, 113, 127, 136, 152–53
Awareness, 14, 27, 34, 35, 37, 39, 40, 43–44, 49, 52, 62, 63, 70, 72, 73–75, 76, 77–81, 82, 83, 86–88, 92–96, 108, 110, 114, 122, 123, 133, 136, 141, 157, 158–59
Balance, aircraft, 23, 51, 100, 155, 158
Balance, sense of. *See* Vestibular system
Bank angle. *See* Turning
Bannister, Roger, 119
Barefoot walking, 33–34
Base leg. *See* Traffic pattern
Baseball, 12
Basketball, 8, 55, 89, 135
Bedding, 143
Bedroom flying. *See* Mental imagery
Behavior, 13, 57, 58, 59, 69, 104, 118
Beliefs, 10, 13, 58, 59, 68, 111, 119–26, 132, 133, 136, 151
Bentley, Ross, 1, 12, 23, 32–33, 67, 82–83, 102–3, 103, 112, 120, 162, 163
Berlin Academy of Music, 90
Berra, Yogi, 12
Big picture, 18, 19
Biographies, 76
Blood alcohol content, 140–41

Index

BMW, 162
Body fat, 139
Body rhythms, 142, 145
Boeing
   737, 69, 163
   747, 163
   767, 87–88
Brain, 9, 12–13, 14, 15, 16, 17, 18–19, 26, 27, 28, 29, 32, 34, 35, 37, 40, 47, 48, 49, 50, 53, 57, 62, 63, 88, 89, 100, 104, 107, 110, 118, 117–18, 138, 141, 159
   Integration, 18–25, 18–25, 26, 32, 112, 124, 133
Brainwaves, 61–63
Brakes. *See* Controls
Briefing, 30, 60, 72, 105, 155, 157
Bruising, 149
Buffet. *See* Stalling
Business, 102, 162
C130 Hercules, 1
Caffeine, 143
Calmness, 25, 100, 102, 108, 114, 133–34, 135, 136
Carbohydrates, 143
Cardiovascular system, 138–40
Career, 1, 9, 11, 81, 113, 133, 134, 152
Carrier pilots, 70
Centering, 23–25, 124
Centerline, 22, 30, 80, 156, 157, 158
CEOs, 162
Challenge, 105, 110–11, 116
Champions, 77, 105, 119–20, 136, 152–53
Checklists, 64, 69, 70, 157, 158
Chicago Bulls, 115
Chocolate, 143
Choking, 117–18
Circuit. See Traffic pattern
Cirrus SR22, 69
Civil aviation, 44, 163
Clean mind, 108
Climbing, 8, 40, 41, 70, 80, 87, 155–56

Coaching, 8, 12, 23, 67, 73, 75, 76, 93, 95, 102, 112, 115, 124, 151, 155–59, 162, 163
Cockpit, 7, 9, 15, 21, 30, 46, 48, 60, 66, 74, 79, 138, 139, 146, 145–49
Cockpit resource management, 106
Cockpit, cardboard, 54, 66
Cognition, 58, 59, 117, 141, 142
Colorado, 114
Combat, 1, 38, 52, 53, 54, 61, 130, 139, 147
Comfort zone, 127–31
Commercial pilots, 44, 52
Commitment, 90, 98, 134, 135, 136, 140, 152
Commonwealth of Nations, 29
Competence, 73–75
Competition, 1, 9, 33, 34, 43, 44, 53, 54, 68, 86, 89, 91, 95, 98, 107, 109, 111–15, 119–20, 120, 121–22, 123, 125, 135, 136, 141, 148, 149, 153
Computers, 13, 14, 19, 49, 64, 68–70, 110, 139
Concentration, 15, 27, 28, 30, 50, 52, 58, 69, 70, 91, 90–91, 99, 105, 106–7, 111–12, 115, 125, 133, 138, 141, 146, 149, 153
Conditions. *See* Atmospheric conditions
Confidence, 13, 58, 59, 68, 83, 96, 99, 102, 104, 111, 117, 122, 125–26, 128, 130, 131–32, 135
Configuration, 15, 34, 35, 36, 40, 42, 66, 79, 94, 156
Confusion, 142
Consciousness, 13, 16, 28, 30, 32, 36–37, 40, 45, 48–49, 49–50, 59, 61–63, 73–75, 76, 82, 83, 88, 104, 106, 107, 110, 113, 114, 115, 117–18, 120, 142, 145, 151
Consistency, 7, 9, 10, 24, 28, 29, 42, 44, 79–80, 80, 81, 84, 95, 100, 106, 113, 119, 120, 132, 134, 148, 153, 156
Contrary evidence, 124–26
Control column. *See* Controls
Controls, 13, 15–16, 33–34, 34, 35, 39, 41–43, 43, 44, 45, 44–45, 49, 50, 54, 57, 59–60, 60, 61, 65–66, 66, 69, 73, 77, 87, 91, 94, 99–100, 104, 130, 137, 138, 146–49, 155, 156, 158

Index

Coordination, 26, 32, 34, 48, 138, 139, 151
Copying, 76–77
Corpus callosum, 19
Cramping, 138–39
Creativity, 18, 19
Crew, 1, 65, 95, 98, 104, 106, 148, 156, 157, 158, 159
Crew resource management, 106
Cross crawls, 19–21, 108, 150
Cross-reference exercises, 44, 70
Crosswind. *See* Atmospheric conditions
Crosswind leg. *See* Traffic pattern
Cruise, 40, 41, 156
Curtains, 143
Cycling, 82, 139
Database, 86–88
Daytona, 162
Debriefing, 70, 73, 92–96, 105, 122, 155–59
Decisions, 13, 97, 101, 135, 140, 141
Dedication, 135
Dehydration. *See* Hydration
Deliberate practice. *See* Practice
Dental surgeon, 33
Depressed, 101
Depression, 125, 142
Depth perception, 14
Descending, 8, 40, 41, 84, 87, 94, 157
Desire, 71, 81, 113, 133, 134, 152
DHC8, 163
Diet, 98, 140, 143, 145
Discomfort, 130
Distractions, 8, 34, 63, 70, 101, 104, 114, 138, 139, 149
Doctors, 61, 138, 140
Dogfight. *See* Combat
Downwind leg. *See* Traffic pattern
Driving, 22, 23, 29, 31, 33, 67, 74, 90, 98, 102–3, 103, 140, 146, 148, 162, 163
Drugs, 140, 143
Durant, Will, 90
Eardrums, 46

Earplugs. *See* Hearing
Eating. *See* Diet
Economy of movement, 109
Edge 540, 69
EEG, 61
Effort, 50, 72, 76, 98, 109, 111, 151, 152, 153
Electroencephalograph, 61
Elephants (pink or blue), 103–4
Emergency. *See* Abnormal
Emotions, 58, 59, 66, 67, 101, 102, 108, 126, 133, 136
Empathy, 101
Endurance, 137, 138, 137–38, 138
Energy
    Aircraft, 36, 38, 61, 86, 105
    Personal, 96, 102, 108, 116, 135, 136, 142, 146, 153
    Engine, 15, 34–35, 38, 39, 52, 59, 64, 66, 108, 147, 155, 158
Engine-out. *See* Abnormal
England, 76
Entertainers, 109
Enthusiasm, 101
Entry parameters, 80, 81, 156, 157
Envelope. *See* Limits: Aircraft
Errors, 8, 15, 22, 28, 37, 35–38, 50, 51, 60, 76, 84–86, 89, 91, 94, 103, 104, 106–7, 110, 113, 116, 121, 125, 131, 133, 141
Europe, 146, 162
Eustachian tubes, 46
Examiners, 93, 111, 112, 111–12, 115, 117, 121
Excellence, 90, 124
Excitement, 101, 108
Exercise, physical, 20, 23, 98, 108, 138, 140, 143
Exertion, 139
Expectations, 114–15, 117, 134, 135, 153
Experience, 7, 8, 9, 16, 36, 37, 41, 76, 87, 91, 94, 95, 98, 110, 127, 128, 129, 131, 133, 134, 147, 162
Eye mask, 143

Index

Eye position, 148
F-16 Fighting Falcon, 147
F-35 Lightning II, 69
FAA, 44
Facilitator, 67
Factual, 18, 19
Failure, 51, 109, 110, 113–14, 116, 133
Failure, fear of. See Fear of failure
Failures. See Abnormal
Family, 116, 117
Fasting, 145
Fat, 139
Fatigue, 108, 138, 142
Fear, 101, 132–34
Fear of failure, 51, 116, 133
Federal Aviation Administration, 44
Federer, Roger, 119–20
Feedback, 30, 31, 33, 37, 39, 40, 44, 66, 79, 85, 95, 133, 146, 147
Feel. See Senses
Feelings. See Emotions
Feet, 16, 33, 49, 66, 146, 147, 148
Ferrari, 90
Fighter pilots, 1, 43, 44, 52, 54, 61, 70, 129, 137, 139, 148
Final leg. See Traffic pattern
Finance, 37, 38, 162
Finesse, 85, 130
Fire-resistance, 139, 148
Fires. See Abnormal
First Officer, 93
Fitness, 89, 137–40
Fitness tracker, 142
Fittipaldi, Emerson, 67, 162
Flaps. See Configuration
Flare. See Landing
Flexibility, 137–39
Flight deck. See Cockpit
Flight engineer, 163
Flight path, 24, 27, 87
Flight Safety Australia, 61
Flight simulator. See Simulation
Flight tests. See Tests
Flow, 19, 110–11, 117, 159
Flying hours. See Experience
Flying instructors. See Instructors
Flying schools. See Schools
Foam-rolling, 138, 144
Focal point, 14
Focus, 31, 52, 58, 67, 69, 73, 89, 99, 100, 101, 103–5, 107, 108, 110, 111–14, 114–15, 116–17, 117, 133, 134, 135, 136, 152, 153, 162
Fokker F27, 163
Football, 8
Forced landings, 52, 66, 83, 133
Formation flying, 60, 91
Formula One, 67, 90, 98, 147, 148
Friends, 98, 116, 117, 151
Fuel, 97, 155, 156, 158
G-
  Force, 15, 27, 38, 39, 43–44, 80–81, 94, 105, 137, 139, 147
  Limit. See Limits: Aircraft
  Load, 39, 43–44, 61, 80, 129, 156
  Meter, 43–44
  Tolerance, 147
Gates. See Reference points
Gauges. See Instruments
Gear. See Configuration
General-aviation, 9, 91, 163
Glare, 149
Glare shield, 40, 148
Glideslope, 24, 40, 70, 84, 157
Gliding, 1
Goals. See Objectives
Go-around, 59, 64, 78, 157
Golf, 55, 56, 89, 90, 100, 120
Grands Prix, 90, 98
Gretzky, Wayne, 89, 98
Gym, 90
Habits, 9, 30, 45, 50, 63, 74, 85, 89, 90, 99–100, 137, 141, 142, 144, 145

- 167 -

Index

Hall, Matt, 61
Hallucinations, 142
Hands, 16, 26, 32–33, 34, 42, 44, 49, 66, 71, 110, 118, 139, 142, 146
Happiness, 101, 102, 125
Harness. *See* Safety equipment
Head, 7, 31, 43, 61, 63, 64, 91, 95, 99, 103, 142, 147
Head up display, 70
Headache, 143
Headset. *See* Hearing
Hearing. *See* Senses
    Loss, 45–46
    Protection, 34, 35, 45, 66, 144, 149
Heart, 108, 139, 147
Heat, 137–39, 143
Helmets. *See* Safety equipment
Hercules, 1
Hobby, 102
Hockey, 89, 102
Holding. *See* Approaches
Horizon, 31, 39, 40, 42, 60
Horizontal stabilizer, 8, 128
Hotels, 143, 145
HS748, 163
Hunter College, 55
Hydration, 139–40
Hypnosis, 63, 109–10
Illness, 46, 141
ILS. *See* Approaches
Indianapolis 500, 67
Indy Car, 67, 147, 162
Insomnia, 142, 143
Instructors, 1, 8, 9, 39, 60, 61, 70, 72, 75, 76, 81, 83, 85, 91, 92, 104, 106, 114, 117, 129, 131, 163
Instrument flying, 23, 69, 91, 105, 122, 156, 157
Instrument rating, 70
Instruments, 8, 24, 26, 34, 41–42, 65, 69, 146
Integration. *See* Brain

Intensity, 91, 96, 99, 100, 107–9, 111, 135, 136, 138
Intuition, 18, 19
Investments, 38
Jackson, Phil, 115
Jet lag, 145
JFK, 69
Jordan, Michael, 89, 98, 115, 135
Journals, 93
Judgement, 141
Juggling, 159
Kinesiology, 162
Kingsford-Smith, Charles, 88, 132
Lacrosse, 162
Landing, 22, 27, 29, 36–37, 38, 39, 40, 42, 70, 73, 74, 77–80, 80, 81, 88, 93, 94, 104, 105, 106, 125, 157, 158, 157–58
Langford, Ronn, 12
Language, 18, 117–18
Lazy 8s, 22–23, 28
Learning, 1, 8, 21, 48, 69, 71–91, 95, 107, 118, 133, 151, 152, 153, 158, 162
    Curve, 74, 81–84
    Formula, 77–81, 87
    Stages, 73–75
Legs, 106, 147
Lemon, 56–57, 60, 65
Lessons, flying, 1, 8, 39, 40, 49, 51, 69, 83, 87, 94, 106, 108, 147, 151
Level, 8, 40, 43, 44, 60, 87, 103, 156
License renewal. *See* Tests
Licenses, 51, 93, 100, 137, 138, 163
Limits
    Aircraft, 16, 39, 40, 43–44, 61, 78, 87, 127–31, 132, 137, 138, 155, 156, 157, 158, 159
    Personal, 29, 68, 70, 107, 114, 115, 114–15, 115, 119, 122, 127–31, 133, 146, 147, 158
Load factor. *See* G-force
Localizer, 24, 70
Logic, 18, 19
Managers, 162

Index

Maneuvers, 33, 36, 38, 41, 43–44, 51, 52, 60, 64, 66, 76, 80–81, 85, 86–88, 90, 94, 99, 105, 129, 130, 132, 133, 139, 149, 156–57
Manipulation, 33, 44–45
Mansell, Nigel, 162
Manuals, 60, 70, 88
Massage, 138, 144
Masters (golf), 89
Mastery, 70, 77, 82, 83, 88–91
Math, 12, 18
Media, 116
Medicine, 141, 143, 159
Melatonin, 143
Memory, 10, 36, 43, 61, 117, 141, 158
Mental imagery, 1, 16–17, 30, 41, 51–52, 58, 68, 53–70, 71, 77–81, 86–88, 88, 89, 99, 104, 105, 115, 118, 121–22, 123, 125–26, 129, 130, 133, 134, 135, 153
Mental programming. *See* Programming
Mentors, 77, 133
Metro 23, 163
MI + A = G. *See* Learning Formula
Military, 1, 9, 20, 66, 72, 162, 163
Minima, 69, 156, 157
Mistakes. *See* Errors
Motels, 143
Motivation, 58–59, 67, 68, 81, 83, 91, 90–91, 116–17, 134–35, 135, 136
Motor skills, 69, 118, 140
Motorsports, 23, 33, 98, 102–3, 103, 120, 146, 148, 159, 162, 163
Muscle memory, 41, 42, 66
Muscles, 62, 108, 137, 138, 139, 144
Music, 63, 90, 108, 110
Nadal, Rafael, 120
Napping, 142–43
Narrative, 60–61, 67
Navigation, 69, 70, 128, 155, 156, 157
Navratilova, Martina, 89
Navy, 70
NCAA, 115

Nervousness, 59, 96, 98, 101, 108, 130, 141
Neural pathways, 47–48, 61, 79
Neuro-linguistic programming, 109
Neuroscience, 162
Noise, 45, 141, 144, 149
Non-normal. *See* Abnormal
Nutrition, 137, 140
Objectives, 59, 71–73, 77, 79, 80, 81, 83, 85, 87, 92–96, 103, 107, 112, 113, 114, 116, 131, 132, 133, 134, 135, 158
Odors, 149
Olympics, 55, 116
Osmosis, 76–77
Over-controlling, 88, 104
Padding, 149
Pain, 138, 146, 149
Panic, 132
Parents, 48, 73, 84, 136, 151
Part-task trainers, 54, 63, 66, 68
Passion, 53, 55, 101, 134, 162
Past experience, 121, 132
Pavlov, 65
Performance, 1, 8–11, 12–13, 14, 15, 17, 19, 22, 23, 24, 27, 30, 33, 35, 37, 39, 40, 44, 45, 46, 58, 60, 61, 67, 68, 70, 72, 74, 76, 81, 90, 92, 93, 95–96, 98, 101–18, 120, 121, 122, 123, 125–26, 127–31, 132, 133, 134, 135–36, 137–40, 140–43, 145–49, 150–53, 159, 162
  Aircraft, 16, 23, 40, 44, 127–30, 135, 155
Peripheral vision, 14, 26, 27, 29, 31, 32, 39, 42, 105, 148
Perseverance, 135, 136
Personality, 69, 97
Phase of flight, 36, 39, 40, 41, 42, 43, 45, 60, 88, 93, 106, 108, 155–59
Phase one. *See* Abnormal
Phelps, Michael, 64, 95–96
Philosophy, 90, 127
Phrasing, 65, 94, 95, 104, 105, 109, 122
Physiology, 81, 124, 133, 142

Index

Pitch, 15, 27, 39, 88
Pitts Special, 34, 54
Plateaus, 74, 82, 81–84
Portugal, 98
Possibilities, 58, 109, 115, 153
Potential, 90, 115, 153
Power, 34, 36, 40–43, 49, 84, 88, 94, 156, 158
Practice, 8, 28–30, 32, 33, 34, 36, 42, 45, 50–52, 54, 55, 57, 63, 67, 68, 69, 70, 72, 74, 76, 77, 79, 80, 83, 86, 88–91, 99–100, 104, 107, 109, 117, 118, 124, 131, 133, 135, 151
Precision, 36, 43, 129, 138, 139
Pre-flight, 70, 96, 95–96, 155
Preparation, 1, 7, 51, 52, 53, 61, 69, 94, 97–99, 113, 115, 124, 125, 130, 132, 135, 142, 144, 151–53
Pre-Planned Thought, 104, 107
Pre-playing. *See* Mental imagery
Pressure, 89, 98, 110, 115, 116–17, 117–18, 120, 136
Prioritization, 28, 127, 159
Prisoner of war, 55–56
Problem solving, 117, 141
Programming, 13, 12–13, 15–17, 17, 30, 45, 47–52, 58, 53–70, 74–75, 77–80, 80, 82, 86, 87, 88–91, 99, 100, 107, 108, 109, 110, 113, 114, 115, 117–18, 119–26, 130, 136
Progress, 81–82, 82, 83, 92, 132
Proprioception, 14, 33
Protein, 143
Psyching, 107–8, 135, 136
Psychology, 1, 24, 58, 118, 124, 162
Psychomotor skills, 13, 109, 141
Push-ups, 139
RAAF, 1, 51
Racquetball, 138, 139, 162
Radar, 159
Radiotelephony, 15, 50, 95, 99, 159
Rahal, Bobby, 162
Reactions, 13, 37, 138, 140, 141

Recency effect, 88–89
Red Bull, 8, 53, 61, 132
Reference points, 36–37, 87, 156
Reflexes, 113, 133, 137–40
Relationships, 102, 136
Relaxing, 63, 64, 68, 87, 88, 100, 107–10, 112, 114, 135, 136, 144–45
Renewal. *See* Tests
Reno, 152
Research, 19, 27, 33, 46, 54–56, 61, 76, 113, 116, 118, 119, 140, 142, 143
Results, 10, 12, 72, 94, 101–18, 124, 133, 134–35, 136, 140, 153
Rituals, 95–96, 102, 118, 144
Rolex, 162
Rolling, 27, 39, 48, 64, 66, 84, 100, 157
Roshi, Suzuki, 109
Routine. *See* Ritual
Rudder. *See* Controls
Running, 138–39
Runways, 1, 16, 22, 24, 30, 31, 36, 37, 39, 60, 73, 77–80, 88, 94, 103, 105, 129, 130, 155, 157, 158
Saccades, 32
Sacred Hoops, 115
Sacrifices, 135
Safety equipment, 66, 98, 137, 147–49
Safety pilot, 129
Scans, 27, 70
Schools, 21, 68, 75, 90, 135, 136, 163
Schumacher, Michael, 90, 98
Science, 162
Scientists, 33, 119, 142, 145
Seat belts. *See* Safety equipment
Seat time. *See* Experience
Seating, 15, 39, 81, 146–48, 149
Sector entries. *See* Approaches
Self-coaching. *See* Debriefing
Self-talk, 122, 125
Senna, Ayrton, 98
Sensations, 43, 126

Index

Senses, 65, 140
  Auditory, 14, 15, 27, 28, 31, 32, 34–35, 43, 45–46, 65–67, 68
  Kinesthetic, 14, 15, 27, 28, 31, 32–34, 39, 43, 65, 66, 68, 87
  Olfactory, 14, 28, 31, 34, 65
  Taste, 14, 28, 31, 34, 65
  Visual, 14, 22, 28, 27–32, 65, 66, 68, 118
Sensitivity, 7, 24, 25–45, 69, 138, 147
Sensory deprivation, 28
Sensory immersion, 65–67
Sensory information, 86–87
Sensory input, 14, 15, 25–46, 27–32, 32–34, 37, 35–38, 39, 38–40, 25–46, 64, 86–87, 151
Sensory perception, 146
Sensory protection, 45–46
Sequences, 8, 16, 36, 38, 39, 51, 52, 54, 57, 59, 60, 61, 64, 65, 64–65, 66, 67, 70, 83, 86, 95, 99, 105, 114, 115, 125, 126, 139, 156
Serotonin, 143
Shift work, 141, 142, 143
Shoes, 33–34, 56, 148
Shorts 360, 163
Shoulders, 23, 147, 149
Simulation, 8, 34, 35, 39, 40, 51, 60, 64, 66, 68–70, 72, 77–80, 87–88, 89, 94, 99, 106, 111, 115, 120, 124, 125–26, 138
Situational awareness. *See* Awareness
Skiing, 106, 114, 163
Sleep, 34, 61–63, 68, 140–45
Smoking, 140, 143
Soccer, 102, 117
Software, 12–13, 15–17, 110
Solo, 24, 72, 107, 108
Soviet Union, 55
Speed, 16, 22, 28, 34, 35, 36, 38, 39, 40, 44, 49, 51, 59, 60, 80–81, 87, 94, 104, 128, 129, 155, 156, 157, 158
Spoilers. *See* Configuration
Sport, 53, 54–56, 58, 99, 102, 108, 110, 114, 118, 119, 121, 132, 135, 136, 138–40, 151, 152, 159, 162

Sport aviation, 139
Sports Cars, 103, 162
Squash, 138, 139
SR-71, 128
Stairmaster, 139
Stalling, 15, 44, 91, 129, 130
Stamina, 149
Standard operating procedures, 97, 99
Star Wars, 110
State of mind, 13, 58, 59, 61–63, 68, 69, 96, 101–18, 126, 132, 136
Stick. *See* Controls
Stick time. *See* Experience
Stimulation, 75, 144
Straight and level. *See* Level
Strength, 137–38
Stress, 1, 24–25, 63, 83, 101, 112, 115, 116–17, 124, 129, 130, 142, 143, 144
Stretching, 138, 144
Student pilots. *See* Trainees
Subconscious. *See* Consciousness
Success, 8, 9, 10, 58, 68, 71–73, 76, 97, 99, 101–3, 109, 111, 113, 115, 119, 120, 121, 122, 131, 132, 133, 135, 136, 137, 152–53, 159
Sullenberger, Chesley, 8
Sunglasses, 149
Superstars, 53, 57, 71, 90, 150–52
Suppleness, 138
Sweat, 139
Sydney, 88
Systems, aircraft, 49, 50, 69, 159
Table tennis, 32, 139
Tailwinds. *See* Atmospheric conditions
Take-off, 15, 16, 24, 31, 40, 49, 52, 70, 87, 103, 129, 155–56
Talent, 71, 72, 81, 89, 90, 98, 120, 134, 135, 150–52, 159
Task-saturation, 117, 128
Taxiing, 24, 70, 108, 155, 158
TCAS, 64
Television, 46, 76, 144, 145

- 171 -

Index

Temperature, 141, 143, 144, 149, 155
Tennis, 32, 76, 89, 99, 100, 138, 159, 162
Tension, 108, 110, 114, 117, 133, 142, 144
Terrain, 121
Testing officer. *See* Examiners
Tests, 24, 51, 59, 70, 93–94, 95, 99–100, 107, 108, 107–8, 109, 111–13, 114–15, 121–22, 122–25, 132, 133, 141
Thoughts, 108–9, 108–9, 144
Threshold, 78, 79, 88, 105, 106, 158
Throttle. *See* Controls
Thrust, 16, 34, 36, 42, 49, 88
Thrust levers. *See* Controls
Time zones, 141, 145
Tiredness, 89, 106, 138, 146
Touch drills, 54
Touchdown. *See* Landing
Track. *See* Navigation
Traffic, 27, 29, 38, 50, 70, 97, 105, 121, 157, 158
Traffic pattern, 8, 15, 22, 27, 28, 29, 39, 40, 59, 60, 66, 70, 73, 78, 80, 84, 87, 97, 157–58

Trainees, 9, 53, 54, 67, 72, 76, 81, 83, 86, 95, 112, 114, 115, 147
Training wheels, 82–83
Tremors, 142
Triggers, 24–25, 58, 63–65, 67, 69, 102, 107, 108, 109–11, 118, 124, 126, 133
Trying, 40, 86, 88, 109–11, 114, 115
Turning, 15, 22, 23, 29, 40, 41, 42, 43, 44, 49, 60, 80, 84, 86, 87, 100, 128, 129–30, 132, 157, 158
University of North Carolina, 115
Unknown, 52, 86–88
Unser, Al Jr, 162
US Road Racing Championship, 162
USAF, 1
Vestibular system, 14, 15, 20, 23–25, 33, 45–46, 83
Vibrations, 27, 38, 39, 44, 147, 149
Video games, 139
Violin, 90
Virtuosos, 90
Vision, 43, 140, 142
Visual reference, 42
Visualization. *See* Mental imagery
Walking, barefoot, 33–34
Warm-up, 20, 95, 108
Weather. *See* Atmospheric conditions
Weight training, 138
Westwood, Lee, 120
Wheels, 37, 79
White-noise, 144
Wilkes, Phil, 1, 29, 30, 34, 40, 51, 54, 66, 67, 77–80, 83, 86, 93, 162–63
Wimbledon, 76, 89, 99
Wind. *See* Atmospheric conditions
Wind shear. *See* Atmospheric conditions
Windscreen, 30, 42, 73
Woods, Tiger, 89, 90, 98, 119–20
World Cup, 117
World Sports Car Championship, 103
Yeager, Chuck, 8, 132
Yoda, 110
Yoke. *See* Controls

My Notes

My Notes

Printed in Great Britain
by Amazon

Printed in Great Britain
by Amazon